BEHIND THE MOSAIC
ONE HUNDRED YEARS OF ART EDUCATION

BEHIND THE MOSAIC

ONE HUNDRED YEARS OF ART EDUCATION

LEEDS MUSEUMS AND GALLERIES IN COLLABORATION
WITH LEEDS COLLEGE OF ART & DESIGN

PUBLISHED ON THE OCCASION OF THE EXHIBITION
BEHIND THE MOSAIC: ONE HUNDRED YEARS OF ART EDUCATION

ORGANISED BY LEEDS MUSEUMS AND GALLERIES IN COLLABORATION
WITH LEEDS COLLEGE OF ART AND DESIGN TO MARK THE CENTENARY OF
LEEDS SCHOOL OF ART AT VERNON STREET

EDITOR: CORINNE MILLER

DESIGNED BY FARMER DESIGN ASSOCIATES, HUDDERSFIELD
PRINTED BY JW NORTHEND, SHEFFIELD

ISBN 0901 981 680

The Annual Exhibition of Leeds College of Art was held at the City Art Gallery in December 1931. A student lamented in the 1932 College magazine:

Here we basked in the benign smiles of City Fathers; our 'Distinguished Visitor' enlightened our darkness concerning 'Modern Art' and the local 'intelligentsia' expressed a kindly, tepid wonder, at the variety and extent of our exertions.

Alas! How little the public know of these things – of the struggles, sorrows and strife that go to build up an effort such as ours. They have not sat through mental stress and storm in the Perspective Class, when the errant intelligence essayed to chase the 'floating ground line,' or, in anatomical enthusiasm, tried to discover if 'condyle' collaborates with 'clavicle' in the structure of the human frame.

His cries echo down the decades to our own experience of Gallery visiting when we wander through the galleries oblivious to the formal training received by the artists whose work we gaze upon. After all, very few of the artists represented in the collections of the Art Gallery were self-taught.

The centenary of the Vernon Street site has provided an opportunity for the Gallery to continue our historic links with those involved in art education in the City through an exhibition and publication which allow us to reflect on art education over the last one hundred years. By giving a presence to the process of art education in a gallery setting we hope that visitors will take the experience of this exhibition into other parts of the Gallery, enhancing their understanding of the artworks on display.

Exponents of Modernism like Hepworth and Moore received a training at Leeds which would have been familiar to students a century before them, an education reliant on the primacy of drawing. Indeed Diderot in his *L'Encyclopedie* illustrates the *atelier* of the eighteenth century where young artists are shown drawing, from prints, casts and the life model in much the same way. Art educators in Britain rarely challenged this approach until the 1950s when process rather than practice became the dominant mode of pedagogy. Leeds, along with Newcastle, was at the cutting edge of these developments under the inspiring leadership of Harry Thubron. It is fitting therefore to record this revolution in art education at Leeds.

The exhibition and the publication do not seek to provide a comprehensive history of Leeds College of Art and Design which has seen many changes in governance over the century. Instead they offer a glimpse *behind the mosaic*, which features so prominently on the front of the Vernon Street building, and a snapshot of the art training offered within the building.

Presented in a chronological sequence, the essays and recollections of former students provide tesserae that make up this mosaic. David Boswell has charted the events leading to the new school of art building on the Vernon Street site, and provided us with a fascinating account of the structure – much of which is still evident today. He has also set the scene for the training undertaken in the school which underwent only minor modifications until the arrival of Harry Thubron in 1955. The period from the 1920s until the Second World War is recorded through the words of former students and an essay on the sculpture and modelling course which was the starting point for Henry Moore, written by Matthew Withey (Assistant Curator, Sculpture, Leeds Museums and Galleries). Inés Plant a former student and Library Assistant has written about the transformative work of Thubron and his colleagues, while Chris Owen (Assistant Principal, Leeds College of Art and Design) describes the assimilation of Basic Design precepts into the Foundation course which we know today. We are grateful to Norbert Lynton for his introduction, which gives a vivid account of his time at the College and to all those former students who have committed their memories to paper to share with us a student's-eye view of college life.

Corinne Miller 2003

ACKNOWLEDGEMENTS

An ambitious project such as this is dependent on help and
advice from numerous people, and we would like to express our
thanks to the following for their support and commitment
to both the exhibition and the publication:

John Adams, Eric Atkinson, Garry Barker, Leonard Bartle,
Sheel Bharj, David Boswell, Pat Burras, Jack Chesterman,
Ruth Conder, Kate Conlon, Margaret Corbin, Alwyn Joseph Doyle,
Lisa Fieldhouse, Katherine Fryer, Chris Graham, Andy Grayston,
Beryl Hammill, Terry Hammill, Marie Hartley, Stella Herklots,
Elspeth Hodson, Bill Hunt, Derek Hyatt, Michael Jackson,
Sean Kaye, Sonja Kielty, Michele Lefevre, Anne Levitt,
Derek Linstrum, Christian Lloyd, Trevor Logan, Rebecca Lowe,
Norbert Lynton, Margaret McCreath, Sandra McDowell, Jill Morgan,
Rachel Moss, Andrew Naylor, Patrick Oliver, Chris Owen,
Derek Page, Jonathan Phillips, Steve Phillips, Inés Plant,
Benedict Read, Pam Rex, Annabeth Robinson, Chris Royffe,
Dave Russell, Julian Satterthwaite, Maisie Smith, Debbie Snow,
Chris Taylor, Jonathan Taylor, Sylvia Thomas, Elma Thubron,
James Towe, Neil Walters, Edmund Wigan, Matthew Withey,
Chris Wood.

Contents

ILLUSTRATIONS

INTRODUCTION
GETTING ONE'S EYES WASHED AT VERNON STREET

NORBERT LYNTON

Life began when I joined the staff in Vernon Street. Come to think of it, life had begun a couple of times before that: when, aged ten, a shy and monoglot refugee from Berlin, I was dropped into a monastic school near Reading and found myself happily taking root there, in the English language, the social life, the studies, even the sports. Or again, seven years later, when I signed up for evening classes at Birkbeck College, University of London, and, unfocused as ever, was advised to try for a 'BA General' in three subjects, English Literature and History, old favourites, and, for luck, something completely new to me called History of Art, taught by Professor Nikolaus Pevsner. It was all good but it was History of Art that grabbed me. After that, more of it at Britain's H of A powerhouse, London University's Courtauld Institute. Two more years and a proper BA Hons degree later, I arrived at Leeds College of Art with a recommendation from the Courtauld's director, Anthony Blunt. It was 1950 and I was twenty-two.

This was almost a false start: Assistant Lecturer in the History of Architecture in the Leeds School of Architecture, part of the College of Art but trenchantly separate from it though just across the street. For six years I taught French Renaissance architecture to reluctant students, ex-servicemen most of them, whose only thought was to get qualified and start earning. The head of the School held that architecture had died about 1800. It was his duty to produce neo-Georgians. Neither the School nor Leeds felt welcoming: the School itself seemed an island desert, and Leeds was. . . For example: if you wanted to see the end of the film, you'd miss your last tram and face a long dark and often damp walk back to your room in the postman's house. I recall the first Leeds coffee bar: about 1955 I think, but I could hardly afford to use it.

That year life restarted quite dramatically (and nearly ended). I had been trying for jobs. I was interviewed for the post of History of Art Lecturer at Hull University, but the job went to someone else, Malcolm Easton, the Leeds College of Art's History of Art Lecturer and Librarian.

Two consequences: the College of Art suddenly lacked an art historian etc, and I caught polio in Hull's cheapest restaurant. But before that showed, I had been invited to take Easton's place. Harry Thubron and his little team – Tom Hudson and Ricky Atkinson – had arrived to run Fine Art. Tom had spent some time at the Courtauld and thought I might do. Harry said yes, and then too did officialdom, and so I was appointed to teach general art history (Lascaux to Impressionism) and modern art history (twentieth century): no interview. I knew very little about the first and nothing at all about the second. The Courtauld did not teach modern art then and encouraged a proper English sense of superiority to it. There were amazingly few good books to learn the subject from. Anyway, polio called for urgent attention. I had driven down to Cornwall in August to visit the first living artist I ever knew – Trevor Bell, ex-Leeds painting student, now again working in Cornwall after years in the USA. I was carted off to Truro Isolation Hospital (a workhouse + cream and green paint). My wife was told to expect me to return a corpse or at best badly paralysed.

The actual outcome was positive: survival + a bit of physiotherapy + three months' recuperation (reading Proust) = more than just OK, a memorable experience. And so was the teaching that followed, a total contrast with the School of Architecture. I started to build up the minimal library. Post-war books on modern art were just beginning to appear, and I was allowed to chase after them. Soon a large room in Vernon Street replaced the tiny rooms up a steep staircase around the corner, to become a busy and effective library in the care of a professional librarian.

I spent a lot of time in the studios; it felt essential to engage with all that. Harry and Tom, two very different men, together revolutionized the place. Harry, often laughing, sometimes impatient, was a natural radical. He could seem a ruffian and he sometimes used a ribald language all his own. He ignored hierarchies. He scared some of the pre-existing College staff, but several of them became allies once they began to understand him.

He could be most subtle in his recognition of quality in anyone's work, including a wide range of students', and he had an instinct for truthful, routineless action that made him the greatest teacher ever. His appetite for art was infinite, and so was his disdain for the histrionic products that kept art commerce going. Tom was strong and brilliant in his way too. He was soon organizing courses in three-dimensional art, alongside traditional sculpture: work in sheet metal, rods, wire etc, in resin and glass fibres, then also vacuum-formed plastics. Tom was something of a Moholy-Nagy amongst us, demanding the new and nothing but the new. Harry was more complex and poetic, with a lot of Van Gogh and Paul Klee in him. I attended one of his winter schools, with no thought of ever being a painter but hoping to get some insight into the basics of it. For ten days we concentrated on the primary colours, adjusting what came out of the tubes until the colours had equal visual presence, discovering the suave joys of discords, etc. I felt my head being both emptied and refilled as I worked, hour after hour, while my eyes were being washed of all that grown-up blindness.

Harry had no doubt that it was important for all artists to know their history and context. I was probably the first certified art historian to teach full-time in a British art school. There was none of that 1968 nonsense about teaching being patronising (of course it is, depending on how you say it, but it's lots of other things besides). I brought in excellent people from the University up the road, to give stimulating informal lectures of a General Studies sort. Harry demanded work, attention, open minds. I got very excited about Klee and his way of letting art grow organically; I could read his diaries before they were translated and used them in teaching and writing a little book about him. Discovering Piet Mondrian was close to a Road-to-Damascus conversion: those brilliant, potent abstracts he called Neo-Plasticism, and the beautiful paintings he did on the way to them! In 1956 and 1959 the 'New American Painting' arrived at the Tate and was nagged at by almost all UK critics. They were no problem to us or to me. But then we had a sequence of powerful new artists coming to Leeds, the Gregory Fellows of Leeds University, who gladly came down the College to be with Harry & Co and did some teaching for us: Terry Frost, Alan Davie and Hubert Dalwood. 'Nibs', as everyone called him, was an impressive sculptor and the funniest man I have ever known, especially when his old friend

ABOVE AND RIGHT: TWO DETAILS
OF THE VERNON STREET BUILDING
BY DAVID BOSWELL
© DAVID BOSWELL

John Jones, teaching in the University's art department, was with him. Nibs talked me into taking my first shot at art criticism in 1959, when he had an exhibition in his studio. After my move to London, in 1961, to run Art History and Complementary Studies at the reborn Chelsea School of Art, I became London correspondent for *Art International* and subsequently also the *Guardian's* art critic.

To summarize it all: London University gave me Art History, and it fascinates me still; but Leeds opened me to art. I shall always be grateful. I write this in the awareness of the many other people who, as students of art and as working artists, have benefited from what Harry and his colleagues launched from Vernon Street. My account is egocentric because that is the only account I can give, but the experience I am speaking of was always outgoing, generous, infectious. It changed the world.

Norbert Lynton 2003

Arts with Crafts

A New School of Art for Leeds

David Boswell

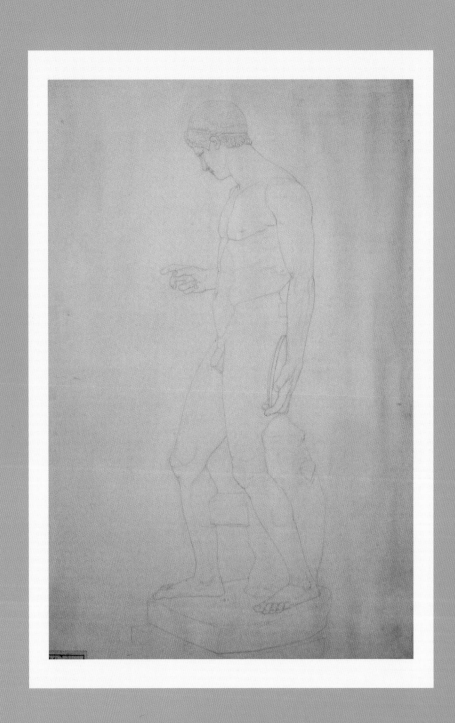

ARTS WITH CRAFTS

BATTLES OVER BRITISH ART EDUCATION AND THEIR IMPACT ON LEEDS INSTITUTE'S SCHOOL OF ART

AVID BOSWELL

The design of the new Leeds School of Art in 1901 attempted to combine long-accepted methods, which gave priority to the skills of draughtsmanship, and modelling with a renewed emphasis on practical crafts. This fulfilled the aims of the Leeds Institute for Science, Art and Literature when they appointed Haywood Rider as Headmaster in 1889, which were fully achieved in the decade before the First World War. In doing so Leeds was in the vanguard of the Schools of Art that imbibed and implemented the philosophy of the Arts and Crafts Movement.

Since its inception in 1836-7 British public education in art had been a battleground of competing aims, methods and ideas. Scarcely had one regime been established than it was undermined and overturned by another. And yet, with certain major differences, the methods of teaching persisted. Art was seen as a craft, with specific skills of observation, dexterity and composition, to be learnt by the repeated application of basic principles before any student could move on to the more advanced stages in which the production of artists might begin. Quentin Bell, Stuart Macdonald and Christopher Frayling have unravelled how the Schools of Design were created, then the Schools of Art, and the transformation of the National, or Central, School into the Royal College of Art, but there have been fewer attempts to trace these through provincial Schools and the climates of local artistic opinion.[1]

The British Government Schools of Design, which followed the foundation of the National Central School at Somerset House in 1837, were not intended to extend the Royal Academy's formal mode of producing fine artists, nor to supplant the many local drawing masters schools. They were to improve the competitive quality of British industrial design. One of their chief proponents, Benjamin Haydon (1786-1846), had the much wider aim of raising national taste and advocated teaching centred on drawing from classical casts and the life model. But the curriculum William Dyce (1806-64) introduced was based on elementary geometrical and freehand drawing in outline and shadowing, from the round (casts) and from nature (especially plants but later the life model), and modelling from the Antique (casts) and from nature. This was followed by a study of ornamental art, seen through the historic styles as differentiated by Owen Jones in *The Grammar of Ornament* etc.[2] Specific instruction in design for different types of manufacture was supposed to follow but proved less popular and uneconomic.

In 1846 the Leeds Mechanics' Institute and Literary Society opened its School of Design, which became a School of Art after further Government reorganisation in 1852, and moved into Brodrick's new Institute building in 1868.[3] For the next half century British art education was to be run from South Kensington by the Department of Science and Art, with Sir Henry Cole (1808-82) as Secretary and Richard Redgrave RA (1804-80) in charge of the National (Central) Art Training School until 1873 and 1875 respectively. Simultaneously drawing lessons were introduced into elementary schools for the poor, and the reconstituted

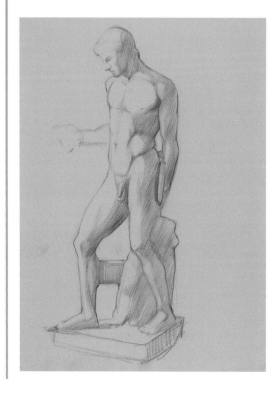

local Schools of Art and the Central School took on the training of art teachers and masters to meet demand.

With periodic modifications Cole and Redgrave's National Course of Instruction effectively remained in operation until its elaborate centralised system became unworkable during the First World War. The course consisted of twenty-three stages. The first ten comprised the Drawing Course devoted to ornamental and linear drawing, freehand outlines from flat reproductions such as the Trajan scroll, and then from casts of the same obtainable at half-price from South Kensington. Shaded drawings from these casts and sketching them within set times, and from memory, followed. The next five stages were devoted to figure and flower drawing, in outline and with shading, from Antique casts. Even anatomical studies were modelled and drawn within the outlines of such cast figures as the Discobolus of Myron, but flowers and objects of natural beauty were permitted because plant forms were considered the basis of almost all ornamental design.

The elementary courses were intended to instil a facility in draughtsmanship, both freehand and mechanical, and accurate observation and representation, which constituted an artistic craft, based on the classical figure and ornamental foliate forms. These continued in the four stages of the Painting Course, which graduated from monochrome to colour, and from text book plates to casts, from cut flowers and pot plants to still life composition, and from plates of human figures and animals to nude and draped life models. There were four similar stages to the Modelling Course. The timed sketches in clay were to encourage rapid perceptions of form and composition, stance etc as different from the elaborate three-dimensional stippled reproductions that could be painstakingly produced over many months for examination submission.

The final group of Design courses could be split between the more advanced art schools and South Kensington. National Scholarships were available, awarded on the results of the National Competition which reassessed the best entries from all the work submitted for examination. The Schools of Art thereby competed for the award of medals: Queen's (King's) prizes and book prizes and Owen Jones prizes for the best designs in applied and decorative

arts awarded by the (Royal) Society of Arts. Additional courses were provided for those intending to teach in the growing number of elementary schools or become art masters in the higher secondary and art schools. Pupil teachers could be appointed as assistants whilst still students in their own School and this became the means of providing higher levels of study at very low rates of pay. Cole's aim was to develop a self-financing system with students' fees as the main source of provincial school finance. The Department of Science and Art gave discounts on equipment, such as plaster casts and illustrated plates and books ordered from South Kensington, and staff were paid 'on results', with a small salary augmented by a percentage based on the number of students enrolled, and their success in the examinations.

Once Cole and Redgrave had resigned, the next Art Director EJ Poynter RA (1836-1919), concentrated on direct drawing from casts and nude life models, elementary anatomical studies, and limited Design to Greek drapery and ornamental motifs. This was criticised by the Royal Commission on Technical Instruction and his successor from 1881 to 1897, Thomas Armstrong (1832-1911), became increasingly well-disposed towards design teaching although the Central School became even more of an art teacher training college. The Arts and Crafts Movement had become a significant alternative source and centre of ideas on design, with the foundation of the Art Workers' Guild in 1884 and the Arts and Craft Exhibition Society's first show in 1889. In the same year, the Technical Instruction Act encouraged the development of technical schools and instruction related to industrial trades and materials, and Design was back on the Schools of Art agenda.

This context shaped the development of Leeds School of Art during Haywood Rider's headmastership from 1889 to 1922. The Institute dismissed his predecessor Andrew Stevenson, after fifteen years in post, following critical reports by the South Kensington art inspector who told the Sub-Committee, 'it was desirable that there should be more teaching of design in the School.'[4] Rider was recommended by the Department of Science and Art. He had National School Master's Certificates in five groups of courses and had been teaching drawing at the Royal College of Science and lecturing at the Central School. He was offered a salary of £150 per annum, one third of the income from fees and payment on the results. In 1889 the Leeds School had 591 students of whom 77 women and 134 men attended its evening classes and 180 girls and 136 boys were taught in the Institute's Technical and Modern schools. In total 297 students had entered the exams but only won two medals and three Queen's prizes. 'The Committee hoped that under the new arrangements the School will be raised in position, and at the end of another year satisfactory results will be rewarded.'[5]

The strategy paid off because by 1892 the total exam results had risen to 625, the highest since the School began, and a branch school opened in Headingley at the suggestion of JE Bedford, one of the new Directors of the Institute who had joined the School of Art Sub-Committee. 'The teaching staff. . . has been strengthened by the appointment of thoroughly competent assistants and teachers of special subjects in applied art *viz.* design as applied to manufactures, lithography, repoussé, etching and woodcarving.'[6] The art and design masters were gold medallists and their assistants were usually drawn from the most successful students such as FH Simpson, CB Howdill ARIBA who set up the courses in architecture and building construction, and E Caldwell Spruce (c.1866-1922) who taught modelling. Spruce had a massive workload as the principal designer of Burmantofts Potteries, but he taught for at least 1891-93, while he was also sitting a series of exams in modelling and design, winning prizes in the National Competition and a free studentship from the School. He was later to compare his own experience of English art education unfavourably with that offered at the Académie Julian: 'In France there is always the feeling of the utter absence of red-tapeism and school discipline. The British student must not sing. He must not smoke. He sits in an infants' school. He works under restricted conditions, with the result that his work is stilted.'[7]

In 1894 two of Spruce's students, Hannah Hunt and Inez Laws, designed and modelled two large panels of *Helios and the Four Winds* for the Sun Fire Insurance building in Park Row.

By 1893 the inspector's report noted that Rider had raised Leeds School of Art 'from an inferior position to one amongst the leading schools in the country', a reputation maintained until the First World War.[8] In 1899 eleven

medals were won in the National Competition. HE Simpson (c.1872-1947), soon to be Rider's long-term Master of the Design Department, won a gold medal for his design for the decoration of a room as well as a bronze medal and an Owen Jones Prize. The Government bought the work of six students from Leeds for demonstration purposes. Walter Crane (1845-1915), the new Principal of the recently restyled Royal College of Art, visited and wrote that he was 'very pleased with the work and especially with that in the Design Room', [9] an assessment repeated by the inspector a year later. In 1900, with thirty National Competition awards, Leeds stood third in the country. Twenty-two of these were in Design compared with six of the eighteen won in 1899. Students' applied artwork also won awards in the local Arts and Crafts Exhibition, and a silver medal at the Paris International Exhibition. Ex-students were by now finding senior teaching posts in other Schools of Art, and the foundation was laid for Leeds' dominant position as a training ground.

The Annual Report of the Institute placed these developments in the context of national policy changes in art education and noted:

The Board of Education now recognise the importance of facilities being given for carrying out a design in the material for which the design or study is intended to be executed, and it is thought the necessity of the association of arts and crafts will be further acknowledged and more strongly insisted on in the future. The practical work of the students will undoubtedly be greatly developed when the new building is erected. In the meantime, it is gratifying to know that the applied art work, now being executed, is such as to merit awards of an exceptional character.[10]

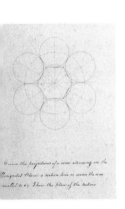

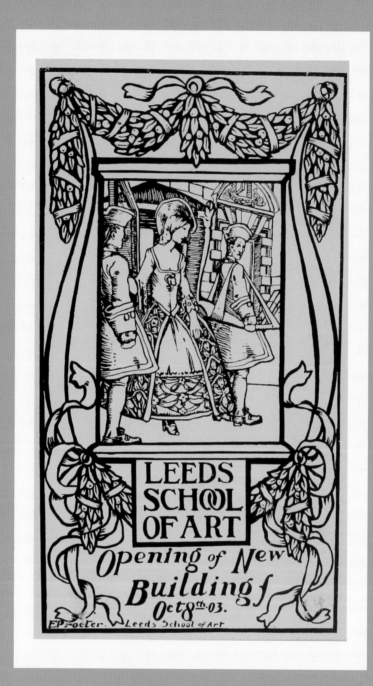

The late 1890s and early 1900s saw a great change in the teaching and practice of the arts in Britain. At the RCA Frayling noted that 'the Art Workers' Guild takes over' and the new Schools of Art at Birmingham (1883-84) and Glasgow (1896-99) were soon extended to introduce practical craftwork in their design courses.[11] Although no craftsman himself, Rider was clearly charged with initiating similar developments at Leeds. The Arts and Crafts fraternity agreed that 'the same deadly dullness had spread over the art teaching of the whole country which centred on South Kensington'[12] and Walter Crane embarked on a series of books on design to drive the debate forward.

In 1899 the opportunity for change arrived when the Board of Education took over the Department of Science and Art and immediately appointed an advisory Council on Art with four Art Workers' Guild members, including TG Jackson and Crane. Professors were appointed to the four main fields of study. Mural and Decorative Painting, Architecture and Design were all headed by Guild members, and Edward Lanteri (1848-1917) was retained to continue his sculpture teaching which had produced many of the 'New Sculptors'. WR Lethaby (1857-1931), Professor of Design, had already embarked on a model for integrating craftwork with art teaching at London's Central School for Arts and Crafts, with a new building to open in 1908. Augustus Spencer (1860-1924), the new RCA Principal until 1920, was to receive many students from Leeds who came to take the Diploma of Associateship. From its inception in 1897 Rider restyled himself ARCA.

In Leeds the ideas and products of the Arts and Crafts Movement were familiar to the new generation of well-educated children of its businessmen and industrial proprietors. Some were returning to the professions like the architects Francis W Bedford (1866-1904) and Sydney D Kitson (1872-1937). Bedford had worked in the offices of WH Thorp followed by George and Peto in London. In 1893-4 The Builder published his Italian sketches from an RIBA Owen Jones Prize, and he became Secretary to

the new Arts and Crafts Exhibition Society in Leeds. His first major commission was Arncliffe, an Arts and Crafts brick house for his elder brother James E Bedford (1855-1927), a keen geologist and collector of early printed books who was a director of the Yorkshire Dyeware and Chemical Co Ltd. In 1897 Bedford formed a partnership with Sydney Kitson who had studied at the Architectural Association and with Shaw's pupil, EJ May. Kitson's half-brother, Sir James (1835-1911), who headed the family locomotive works, was a leading Liberal MP and advocate of technical education.

In 1894 James Bedford took over the chair of the Institute's School of Art Sub-Committee, and with WH Thorp, set out to extend teaching in crafts relevant to local manufactures, develop an architecture department, and provide a new building for the expanding number of students. In November 1900 six local architectural practices were invited to submit, for a fee of £20, plans for a new School of Art to cost no more than £10,000. Several of the architects had studied or were teaching at the School and all were active members of the Leeds and Yorkshire Architectural Society. The Sub-Committee's brief was informed by visits, in the company of the Headmaster, to new Schools of Art where design and craftwork played a significant part, such as Glasgow, Birmingham, and in London, the schools at Regent Street, Camberwell, Battersea and the Royal College of Art.

The Vernon Street site was a constricted one, behind the Institute's main building and flanked by the Institute's Boys' and Girls' Modern Schools on Rossington Street. The Institute already owned the land but a gymnasium would be required because these schools had lost their playground. Thorp drew up the Instructions which required plans of each floor, four elevations, one longitudinal and two transverse sections, and a block plan of the site. Line drawings only were required and no perspective, except from the competition winner. A building of three floors, over a basement high enough to light applied art work rooms was suggested, with mezzanines for small rooms and services, a lecture room and a bridge to the Institute.

The main entrance should face Cookridge Street, and therefore be seen from the front of the Institute. It was to be lit by electricity but the lift for the casts and modelling clay would be hand-powered. Stress was laid on the need for fresh, as well as warm air. High, even lighting was essential for art classrooms with narrow metal frames for the windows not heavy mullions or transoms. The accompanying *Schedule* suggested the area to be provided for each teaching room and workshop and the preferred floor and orientation needed for each activity. Red Accrington or similar brickwork was specified with neat dressings of Yorkshire stone but, apart from fire-proofed circulation areas and sound-proofed floors, there were no specifications about metal beams etc.

The amount of money available for the erection of the building being limited, and its position situate at the rear of the Institute, an ornate treatment of the exterior is not desired. Competitors are, however, requested to design a building of plain character, which, by its proportions and architectural outline and patterns, will not only harmonise with the existing Institute, but will also look appropriate for its intended use. The interior should also be of a plain and simple character, and all plaster and other mouldings liable to catch and retain dust are to be carefully avoided.[13]

It was absolutely clear that no terracotta gothic showpiece like the Birmingham School, which cost £20,000, was required. But the choice of WH Bidlake MA (1861-1938) as the competition's assessor is significant. An acclaimed architectural student at the RA Schools and GF Bodley's

practice, his notable Arts and Crafts Gothic church of St Agatha's, Sparkbrook, was just completed and in 1899 he had designed a branch School of Art in Moseley. By 1901 he was developing the teaching of Architecture in Martin and Chamberlain's new School at Birmingham. Bidlake had:

. . . no hesitation in recommending No 4 [the submission of Bedford and Kitson] as the best arranged, the most economical in first construction and subsequent working and presenting the best external elevations. . . The general lines of this plan are simple and direct; the various parts lie in natural relationship with each other; there are no narrow or ill-lighted passages or corners liable to a congestion of traffic; and the lighting is carefully studied. . . There is an air of sincerity in the design of the large windows with steel lintels which is pleasing.[14]

With the exception of this last stylistic evaluation, Bidlake's comments were about function. He accepted the provision of less space for workshops and more for Light and Shade and Modelling than in the *Instructions*. But he had several specific criticisms. The subsidiary staircase should be extended to the basement entrance as a fire escape. Direct heating of the life rooms would be an advantage. Some small rooms could be extended such as the plasterer's room by taking in the space under the front steps. Each room needed its own access door. The lecture room could be more effectively raked by cutting into the floor below, and the life rooms on the second floor needed more light.

In the Building Plans lodged with the local authority and dated 23 August 1901, almost all these modifications were implemented and today the School still essentially serves the purposes for which it was built. Since the 1960s there have been three major structural changes: the replacement of the Gymnasium by three floors of studios over a canteen; the conversion of the Light and Shade Room into a library and, since 1993, the erection of galleries in several studios and use of common rooms for staff offices. Even by the time the first plans were published in the Institute's *Calendar and Syllabus*, alternative accommodation had been found for the large Painting and Decorating class and Architecture soon followed.[15]

The designation of the School's main rooms and their position follow South Kensington's curriculum requirements. Elementary teaching was on the ground

LEFT: INTERIOR OF THE VERNON STREET BUILDING (DETAIL) BY DAVID BOSWELL © DAVID BOSWELL

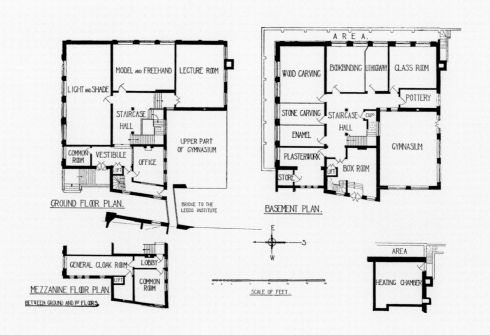

GROUND FLOOR PLAN.

LIGHT AND SHADE
MODEL AND FREEHAND
LECTURE ROOM
STAIRCASE HALL
UPPER PART OF GYMNASIUM
COMMON ROOM
VESTIBULE
LIFT
OFFICE
BRIDGE TO THE LEEDS INSTITUTE

BASEMENT PLAN.

A R E A.
WOOD CARVING
BOOKBINDING
LITHOGRAPHY
CLASS ROOM
POTTERY
STONE CARVING
STAIRCASE HALL
CUPD
ENAMEL
GYMNASIUM
PLASTERWORK
STORE
LIFT
BOX ROOM

MEZZANINE FLOOR PLAN.
BETWEEN GROUND AND 1ST FLOORS.

GENERAL CLOAK ROOM
LOBBY
LIFT
COMMON ROOM

E
N
W
S

SCALE OF FEET.

AREA
HEATING CHAMBER

FIRST FLOOR PLAN.

PAINTING
ARCHITECTURE
DESIGN ROOM
STAIRCASE HALL
ELEMENTARY MODELLING
LIFT
MALES LAVATORY

SECOND FLOOR PLAN.

LIFE ROOM
ANTIQUE ROOM
MODELLING
MASTER'S ROOM

MEZZANINE FLOOR PLAN.
BETWEEN FIRST AND SECOND FLOORS.

LADIES LAVATORY
LIFT

E
N
W
S

SCALE OF FEET.

THIRD FLOOR PLAN.

FAN
CONSERVATORY
MASTER'S STUDIO

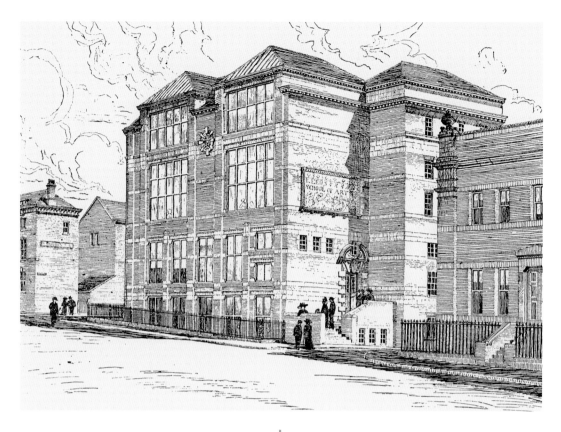

LEFT: THE NEW SCHOOL OF ART
PEN AND INK PERSPECTIVE BY
GEOFFREY LUCAS, NOVEMBER 190[
LEEDS INSTITUTE CALENDAR 1904
COURTESY OF LEEDS LIBRARIES

floor and the advanced life drawing and modelling and antique cast rooms at the top, with more specialised departments between. The modelling rooms were stacked near to their source of clay by the lift. And the Headmaster had a suite at the top with a penthouse studio and conservatory, like Glasgow, for the plants needed for drawing from nature. Like Glasgow, basement provision was made for a wide range of craftwork.[16]

As Bidlake observed, the structure and elevations are easily explained by these internal functions. Unlike the other new schools, Leeds had no wide street frontage, so Bedford and Kitson wrapped the rooms around the south-lit central staircase hall with the main entrance, facing Cookridge Street, beneath and to one side of the stack of mezzanine floors. This hall is steel-framed and every floor is supported on RSJs with floor surfaces related to room function. Although the fenestration differs between floors, each elevation has a uniform composition. Extra light was acquired for the basement and the north lights on the first floor by the use of dormers forming bulkheads in the floor above. But on the top floor, the sloping roof over each window was glazed instead. Slender steel glazing bars were used throughout and the riveted girders over the main windows were left exposed. Even the rusticated bulls-eye on the Vernon Street front served a purpose – to light the life-models' changing cubicles (not shown on the Syllabus plans). And the mass of little mezzanine windows, although given a balanced distribution, was effectively concealed behind the bulk of the Institute.

Often typified as an Arts and Crafts design, the term Free-Style coined by Hermann Muthesius, the Prussian art official who commended both Bidlake's, and Bedford and Kitson's house designs, seems more appropriate.[17] Although built in a much brighter brick and lighter Ancaster stone than the Institute, the extensive use of horizontal stone courses visually modifies the School's greater height and the vertical thrust of its tall window bays. With the cornices and shallow buttresses they subdivide the elevations and are neatly detailed. The exposure of the steel window lintels was a functional statement as well as an economy, and not repeated in the offices and public buildings of the practice such as the Leeds Public Dispensary of 1902-4. The main entrance, however, which

Bidlake considered 'somewhat insignificant', was given emphasis by heavy rustication and a large, colourful, stone-framed mosaic designed by Professor Gerald Moira (1867-1959) of the RCA and made in Rust's patented vitreous mosaic.

As soon as Bidlake's report was discussed, a Building Sub-Committee, run by James Bedford and Thorp, was set up. Geoffrey Lucas provided a pen and ink perspective of the new School which was reproduced on the appeal leaflet.[18] The cost was estimated at £12,000, part of which would be covered by a mortgage of the Institute. Chas. Myers and Sons were awarded the building contract and Sir James Kitson laid the foundation stone on 11 December 1901, using the occasion to outline the threat from American competition and the need for technically instructed recruits to industrial management.[19] By 1905 the Building Fund had raised £1,837 15s 0d.

Francis Bedford and Sydney Kitson often attended Sub-Committee meetings to discuss progress and small modifications. But one of the last tasks was the estimate for equipping the School with furniture, screens and panelling, put out to tender in March 1903.[20] This included 100 stools, 16 figure and bust stands, 13 blackboards to slide into boxed casings and one blackboard wall 240 feet long, and a platform for the master's desk, 120 desks and chairs from a Glasgow firm, 52 easels, and a throne and screen for the model to undress behind. A furnace and enamelling equipment were purchased together with a male skeleton for modelling. Thorp and Rider drew up lists of antique figure and architectural casts and Musto

the lantern slides for Architecture. Moira's mosaic was paid for by Sampson Fox.

Andrew Carnegie was invited to open the new building, no doubt in hope of a substantial contribution to the Fund, but it was the Honorary Treasurer, Ernest W Beckett MP, who actually did so on 8 October 1903. In an address, printed in an edition of 1000, he castigated the City Council for failing to support technical education, praised the students for results that attracted the highest School of Art grant in the country, and the provision of Fine Arts with Arts and Crafts instruction so that what the student 'learned in the studio he can execute in the workshop. The theoretical and the practical go hand in hand.'[21] A *conversazione* followed for 800 guests, hosted by James and Mrs Bedford. Students of the Schools of Music and Art combined in a concert programme with tableaux arranged by Alfred Rushton, just back from the RCA. The allegorical figures dressed as trees, flowers, leaves and fruit recall the diaphanous costumes that Walter Crane designed for such occasions. A student, Ernest Procter, designed the elegant programme cover.[22]

ELEVATION to the scale of ¼ inch to 1ft.
showing height from ground the ceiling is fixed.

modern plaster frieze

Full size section
of the beading.

PLAN, looking up, Scale ¼in to 1ft.

While the new School was being built the Education Act of 1902 was passed which, together with associated Acts, was to transform the provision of English education. The responsibilities of the School Boards were passed to local authorities along with technical and higher levels of secondary education. The RCA was separated from the Department, and the Board of Education began to phase out payment on results. But for several years the Institute remained responsible for its new School, with local junior and senior scholars attending full-time from Leeds and the West Riding. HE Simpson had his salary increased as Design Master and two prize-winning students in metalwork and enamelling, and in textile design, THE Abbott and Clara Lavington, were appointed assistant teachers of design. Specialist teachers were appointed to teach bookbinding and woodcarving while further appointments were made to assist with drawing and painting.

The teaching of architecture was given a new impetus when the Leeds and Yorkshire Architectural Society (LYAS) approached the Institute to establish a School of Architecture for the region, nominate the master, and have a seat on the committee.[23] By contrast, after Spruce left, a series of modelling teachers proved unsatisfactory and Rider eventually sought Professor Lanteri's advice, resulting in the appointment of an experienced teacher, Charles H Broughton ARCA in 1904.

The Institute's annual *Calendars*, illustrated by Pickard's photographs of the art rooms in use, provide both a general and a detailed view of how teaching and course provision was developing over the period and the facilities offered in 1904-6, with a syllabus directly based on those of the Board of Education, the City and Guilds of London Institute, and the RIBA, which were the examining bodies.

The objects of the School are to impart by a systematic course of instruction a knowledge of the Principles and Practice of Art, with a view to its application by manufacturers, designers, craftsmen, and all intending to make Art a profession; to form a sound and comprehensive base for the study of its Pictorial and Ornamental branches; and to instruct those who desire to make a knowledge of Art a part of their general education. In the case of Building Construction, Bookbinding and other technical subjects, the aim is to give the student a thorough grasp of every part of his trade or craft.[24]

The course details, often with a description of the form of its exam, indicate how much of the nineteenth century system was still intact. A few examples from more than fifty pages will indicate the sort of ideas underlying teaching and the methods of instruction and examination in different departments. In Architecture 'most important of all. . . is continued and careful study of old buildings and woodwork, both by sketching and measuring. This work is absolutely indispensable to real progress in the architectural profession.'[25] Anatomy included the proportions of the human figure, figures in motion, the skeleton, including such details as the 'haunch-bone as a determinant of form', and the relationship of muscles to expression. Drawing and Light and Shade from casts using pencil, chalk, pen and ink or water colour wash (but not yet charcoal) were examined using plaster casts such as the *fleur de lys* sent directly from South Kensington. Memory Drawing of Plant Form required an anatomical knowledge of a specific flowering plant.

Advanced courses included Drawing and Painting from Life, which were examined by drawings from the nude and from memory. Drawing Common Objects from Memory was examined by drawing an everyday object of choice, such as a tin bath, from different angles and in a composition with two or three other objects. The specified casts for Antique Drawing included the Venus de Milo and the Discobolus. Modelling formed the other main element of the curriculum and its exams set aside a day for plaster casting from the clay model made over several previous evenings. Modelling included studies from the life model and modelling from a skeleton and muscular details from casts.

The Design course had several stages; an elementary exercise fitting different types of ornament into a given

LEFT: MEASURED DRAWING OF A PINEWOOD CEILING FROM THE PALACE AT TORRIJOS, NEAR MADRID IN THE VICTORIA & ALBERT MUSEUM BY ALAN W BELLIS, 1910 PENCIL, WATERCOLOUR AND BODYCOLOUR 72 x 46.8 CM PRIVATE COLLECTION

shape and repeating patterns, an advanced applied design consistent with historic styles but not reproducing an existing model, and an honours level requiring a complete decorative scheme with a panel detailing part of the design at full scale. The exam expected drawings using a watercolour wash and shading but not colourful painting. Plant forms were seen as fundamental to decorative ornament, while the Headmaster lectured on the wide application of Historic Ornament to monuments and buildings, furniture, utensils and personal adornment in primitive and ancient civilisations, the use of different materials in the works of artists and in costume, armour etc. Painting Ornament was a test of the students' ability to create a design in three tones of one colour, in tempera, on a previously prepared canvas based on a diagram or photograph from nature supplied by the examiners.

From the prize awards one can see how the provision of specialist workshops contributed to advanced level designs submitted in their proposed materials such as metal work, enamel or textiles. There were also specific courses in Woodcarving, Enamelling, Embroidery and Lace, Lithography, and Jewellery and Silversmiths' work. City and Guilds' exams were taken in Bookbinding, Cabinet-Making, Painting and Decorating, with Wrought-Ironwork to follow some years later.

The last years in which the Institute ran its schools were 1904-6. When James Bedford relinquished the chair in 1904 to become President of the Institute, he remained a Sub-Committee member with Thorp in the chair. Francis Bedford had just died but Sydney Kitson became Honorary Secretary of the Institute and represented the LYAS on the School's Sub-Committee. When FH Simpson resigned and Alfred Rushton departed to head Hartlepool School of Art, Rider took the opportunity to reorganise the School in 1905 along the lines of the RCA. FW Musto ARIBA headed Architecture, HE Simpson, Gold Medallist, Design. Charles Broughton ARCA had come to head Modelling, and in 1905 WB Pearson ARCA became Head of Life Drawing and Painting on the recommendation of the RCA. It was a very professional team. Percy Teasdale, an established local painter who had studied in Paris, was taken on especially to teach portrait and life painting. Rider was, however, himself censured for failing to fulfil his teaching agreement of 1902 and required to teach more day and evening courses. He was not allowed to be a full-time administrator. Two of the seven assistant teachers, all prize-winning students of the School, were promoted to senior assistants. The crafts programme was extended to include gesso work, mural decoration, pottery and repoussé work, but stone carving recruited too few students and no teacher.

From the prizes won in the National Competition over these years, it is obvious that most were in Design and won by women. Not surprisingly, however, the most popular courses were the core curriculum of Drawing and Modelling with the advanced courses of Painting of Ornament in Monochrome, Memory Drawing of a Plant Form, and Drawing on the Blackboard a necessity for prospective teachers, followed by Painting from Still Life, Drawing the Antique from Memory, Geometrical Drawing, and submissions for Art Masters' and Teachers' Certificates.

The annual exhibitions of students' work at the School attracted between 1,500 and 3,000 visitors, and Rider arranged September exhibitions at the City Art Gallery of the best work shown at the National Competition in South Kensington. From 1891 they could participate in local Arts and Crafts exhibitions, the most ambitious of which was held at the City Art Gallery in 1904. Supported by the Lord Mayor and Mrs Currer-Briggs, patrons of CFA Voysey (1857-1941) and Hamo Thorneycroft (1850-1925), this involved the School of Art, the local branch of the Arts and Crafts Exhbition Society, and the Leeds Arts Club, a radical forum for socialist and Nietzschian ideas founded in 1903, which was to mount significant exhibitions of its own.[26] Art School students could attend public lectures by leaders of the Movement like Lethaby and TJ Cobden Sanderson, and Percy Jowett and Alan Bellis both won awards for their poster designs.

A closer look at a handful of successful students of the new building's first years will illustrate the variety of their studies at the School and their careers in art. First, the Procter brothers from Tyneside whose father came to head the Leather Department at the Yorkshire College. The elder, JC Procter (d1940), began his architectural studies in 1899, passed the Intermediate stage of the RIBA exams in 1903 and the Finals in 1907. He set up his practice in Leeds and was to be closely involved in the Leeds and Yorkshire Architectural Society and its association with the Architectural Department at the School. In 1937-8 Procter designed the new City Library and Art Gallery which was shelved due to the war. His younger brother, Ernest (1886-1935), achieved a first class result in Drawing from Life in 1904 and by 1907 had joined

Stanhope Forbes's School of Painting at Newlyn. There he met Dod Shaw (1892-1972) and they married after both spending a year studying in Paris. Thereafter they divided their time between Newlyn and Coniston, and both were elected to the New English Art Club and the Royal Academy. Several of Ernest's early watercolours are in the collections of Leeds City Art Gallery.[27]

Clara Lavington completed most of her elementary courses and several in Ornament in 1899, winning a book prize. The next year she won a Bronze Medal, a Queen's Prize and a book prize for her lace blouse and scarf design, with first class results in most of twelve other courses, and one work submitted towards an Art Teachers' Certificate. On the strength of this she was appointed an assistant (pupil) teacher in Design. In 1902 she resumed her exam submissions, achieving nine more first class results and a bronze medal for her cretonne design and a book prize for a silver belt clasp. In 1903 her design won a silver medal and was retained from the National Competition to be sent to the International Exhibition at St Louis. After winning another silver medal and an Owen Jones Prize for work in two advanced design courses, she was promoted a Senior Assistant teacher in 1905 and remained on the staff throughout the years of war. Thereafter, as with so many of the women at the School, she seems to disappear from the records but contributed to the College's centenary exhibition in 1946.[28]

Thomas Abbott first came to the School in about 1897 aged sixteen. Born in Australia, he came to Leeds with his photographer father. In the following six years he obtained a book prize for a stencilled hanging and frieze

in 1900, and a bronze medal for a design from a plant form the next year when he was appointed an assistant teacher. He continued with eight or ten successful course results each year, winning a prize in 1902, bronze medal in 1903 for a chalk drawing from the Antique and a King's Prize in 1904. Further bronze medal winning designs were bought for Wellington Art School in New Zealand. He also submitted annual works towards the Art Teachers' and Art Masters' Certificates. Like Clara Lavington he was promoted a Senior Assistant. In 1907 Abbott won the coveted Gold Medal, as had the Head of Design HE Simpson, for his Crucifix in Grisaille enamel. He said he could not afford to experiment in enamel until two years before, and hoped to revive the dead art working in the School's basement.[29]

William Brownfoot (1883 -1949) was working for Gilchrist Printers when he first came to the School. At the early age of thirteen he first took exams in the relatively advanced courses of Drawing from the Antique, Drawing from Life and Painting from Still-Life, all passed with first class results. In the next two years he submitted more Painting from Still-Life and in 1903 won a prize for his lithography (Walter Crane's popular textbook *The Bases of Design*, first published in 1898). After serving on the

Western Front from 1916-18, Brownfoot set up a picture framing business near Leeds Infirmary. A member of every subsequent generation of his family has studied at Leeds School of Art.

These last three were local students who remained in Leeds. By contrast the final pair graduated to the RCA and a career in teaching art elsewhere. Alan W Bellis (1883-1960) came from Manchester when his father was appointed to manage Petty's printing works. He was apprenticed in the trade but, like Brownfoot, really wanted to be an artist and probably became an evening student in 1899. After taking a few courses a year, his proficiency improved in 1901 and, when he won a local scholarship and could study full-time from 1902, his output was prodigious and his results usually first class. Thirteen results that year, eleven the next, and seventeen in 1904, included several works for the Art Masters' and Teachers' Certificates. In 1906 he was bracketed first for the United Kingdom and received the King's Prize for Excellence.

Fortunately a sequence of Bellis's drawings and watercolour designs survive including a sketch of *The Portico of the Chapter House, Kirkstall Abbey* of about 1903, and a measured drawing of the Abbey's Nave

LEFT: JACOBEAN SCREEN FROM THE CHURCH OF ST JOHN THE EVANGELIST, NEW BRIGGATE, LEEDS BY ALAN W BELLIS, 1905 PENCIL AND MONOCHROME WASH 50 x 72 CM PRIVATE COLLECTION

Arcade. These, with a pair of *Full-Size Details of the Pulpit in St John's Church, Leeds*, indicate the types of study and colour-washed drawings produced at the School. His *Measured Drawing of a Sheraton Bergere Chair* was taken from furniture owned by the Headmaster. Two drawings submitted for the Art Masters' Certificate in 1905 are a measured drawing of *The Jacobean Screen from St John's Church, Leeds* and a set of pen-and-ink drawings of *The Classic Orders of Architecture*, taken from the text book by R Phené Spiers, who taught at the RA.

In 1906 Bellis won a Royal Exhibition of £100 per annum to the RCA. In 1911, presumably after a spring vacation in Rome, he won the Owen Jones Prize from the RIBA for a group of drawings of Pope Paul III's chambers at the Castel St Angelo, and carved heraldry in Leeds churches, which were published in *The Builder*. It gave an opportunity to study in Italy, where Bellis spent the year, completing studies of frescoes in Florence and a mosaic vault in Rome. In 1912 he was appointed to teach modelling and metalwork design at Ipswich School of Art and retired in 1948. In 1916, he enlisted in the Artists' Rifles with whom he was captured, spending his imprisonment at Mainz, returning to Ipswich at the end of 1918.[30]

Percy H Jowett (1882-1955) was a contemporary of Bellis but enrolled at a later age, after an education at Harrogate Technical School. He spent three years of intensive study at Leeds, with fifteen results in 1902, ten in 1903 when he won a prize and was awarded a local scholarship, and fourteen in 1904. Each year he submitted several works for the Art Masters' and Teachers' Certificates and won the King's Prize for Drawing in Light and Shade in 1904, when he and Bellis also had success at the Leeds Arts and Crafts Exhibition. Having first class results in every department, he was appointed an assistant teacher but soon left to take up a Royal Exhibition to the RCA in 1904, two years before Bellis. There he won the Prix de Rome and spent a year studying painting. He experimented with the new ideas and forms of painting and became a member of the Seven and Five Group after the War but settled on Cézanne as the main influence on his landscapes and flower paintings, becoming a member of the NEAC and the Royal Watercolour Society. A career in art education took him to head the School of Art at Chelsea Polytechnic and the Central School of Arts and Crafts. From 1935-47 he was Principal of the RCA following the

retirement of Sir William Rothenstein, for whom he had worked in the Leeds Town Hall murals project in 1920.[31]

These were just a few of the students at Leeds who began very different careers in art and art education in the early years of the School's new building. One can see the dominant force of the South Kensington examination system and the elaborate array of prizes, which gave access to scholarships and teaching appointments. One can also see how the introduction of more practical craftwork was incorporated within the same system. The ideas of the Arts and Crafts Movement had been adopted and transformed into a new form of orthodox art education.

Chapter House
KIRKSTALL AB

The Leeds Institute was delighted with the improved conditions for Applied Art in its new school, and the enrolment of 616 students in 1904, but looked to the new Leeds and West Riding Education Committees to provide scholarships for more day boys, and to co-ordinate local facilities for teaching art. By 1905 the implications of the 1902 Education Act had become clear. Under the heading 'No Surrender', James Bedford, the Institute's new President, warned the press of his fears.[32] In 1906-7 the City Council took over all the Institute's buildings and its Technical, Modern, and Art Schools. However a number of Institute nominees retained positions on the management sub-committees, so Bedford, Thorp and Kitson continued to exert their influence on the School of Art.

James Graham, Leeds Secretary for Education, and the Institute soon laid claim to the School of Art in different ways. The City Council published the Board of Education Inspector's Report as an Appendix to its Committee Minutes in 1907-8. Apart from some criticism of lack of workshop space, specialised equipment and an adequate reference library, the systematic curriculum was especially commended:

This is particularly the case in respect of the co-ordination of the technical art work with the study of Drawing, Modelling and Design. All the students in the Embroidery, Jewellery, Bookbinding and Painting and Decorating Sections study drawing and design, and in the first two subjects named, the co-ordination is so complete that these Art Craft subjects might almost be considered as technical branches of the Design Section. The same complete system of co-ordination obtains in relation of the work and painting to other branches of study in Art Crafts.[33]

The inspectors were pleased that most of the twenty Senior Scholars were drawn from the Junior Scholars, ensuring a progressive three- to five-year course. But they were critical of the lack of time specialist teachers had for their own work, of the restricted form of the Architecture courses, and the undue influence of the casts on modelling the nude from life, which required 'a faithful imitation of nature'.

James Graham was anxious to publicise the state of the School under the new regime. He also had his own ideas about art education. He arranged an exhibition in 1908 with Bradford and the West Riding, based on that organised in London for the *International Art Congress for the Development of Drawing and Art Teaching and their Application to Industries*. In his notes and suggestions for teachers he was concerned that the foreign teacher was better trained. 'He is a better workman, with a fuller knowledge of his materials and how to use them to the greatest advantage.' Graham regarded 'memory drawing' as of the most general importance and referred to an experiment which demonstrated the stultifying effects of starting with mechanical drawing and measurement in elementary schools rather than drawing from nature and how this affected pupils' subsequent development in craft work.[34]

The Institute responded to its reduced circumstances with an Old English Autumn Fair to raise funds to refit its remaining rooms. Thorp, who still chaired the School of Art's Sub-Committee, suggested a decorative scheme recreating the Market Place and Old Moot Hall of a century before, which the staff and students 'realised in a most satisfactory manner.'[35] Fred Lawson of the School provided the *Official Handbook and Programme* with a cover design.

During the next few years considerable efforts were made to establish fruitful relationships with local industries, establishing dedicated art craft courses taught by specialist teachers from the trade. Advisory committees were set up in Plastering and Decorating, which had by far the largest number of students, Printing and Allied Trades, Cabinet Making, Jewellery and Silversmithing, Modelling and Pottery, Wrought Ironwork, and of course Architecture.

In 1911, under Sydney Kitson's chairmanship, Architecture produced its own challenging *Prospectus*. The Department had been re-organised by George Coombs, who had both ARCA and RIBA qualifications, and offered courses leading to all levels of the RIBA exams taught at the Methodist

LEFT: PORTICO OF CHAPTER HOUSE, KIRKSTALL ABBEY (DETAIL) BY ALAN W BELLIS C1903 PENCIL AND WATERCOLOUR 20.7 X 25.7 CM PRIVATE COLLECTION

ABOVE: HAYWOOD RIDER (CENTRE)
WITH STAFF AND SOME STUDENTS
AT LEEDS SCHOOL OF ART, C1911
COURTESY OF THE PEARSON FAMILY

Church rooms in Woodhouse Lane. Kitson was President of the LYAS, whose members continued to act as visiting critics, and every effort was made to obtain full recognition of the courses and exemption from the RIBA's Intermediate and other exams. Negotiations dragged on until 1914 when a dialogue was set up with Professor Reilly's Architecture Department at Liverpool University. Exemption from the Intermediate exams was approved the next year but from the RIBA Finals only in 1929.[36] By contrast, it took the Board of Education only two years to recognise the School, also in 1915, as one of only four provincial art schools to be a Centre for Teacher Training, awarding a diploma ranking with its own Teachers' Certificates and the ARCA.

The Advisory Committees were a useful source of prizes for students' work, and a means of obtaining samples of marble, woodwork veneers, paints, varnishes and books from manufacturers. The Trustees of the British Museum donated reproductions of illuminated manuscripts and other objects and several casts of architectural elements and statues in their collection, as did the V & A Museum. Objects for still-life and applied arts studies as well as books and pictures were occasionally bought, but more frequently given by Sub-Committee members and other benefactors; John Ruskin presented a watercolour by William Hunt (1790-1864) in 1859 and Atkinson Grimshaw's widow donated his easel in 1913. James Bedford was a regular donor of books, a panelled settle and numerous examples of oriental and art pottery and metalwork.

Throughout the pre-war years, the School of Art maintained its successful record. Rooms were rearranged to accommodate more art crafts. But as the use of costly materials increased, advice was sought as to who owned student's work. It was generally agreed that it was the School unless students paid for their materials. So it is surprising that virtually nothing remains of the best students' work or any of the artwork donated over the years. Under the City Council, exam results were no longer published in full and few names of award winners appear in the Minutes and Reports. But there is enough to show

the rapid success of the wrought-iron workshop, begun in 1910 under Silas Paul who had studied at the School and had been a gold medallist in the first year. Like the Head of Design, who produced several official chains of office for local dignitaries, Paul also did his own work and in 1913 made the font-cover for St Aidan's Church to Kitson's design.

In addition to the steady stream of RCA scholars, Broughton and Pearson's students also found places at the Royal Academy Schools where tuition was free of charge. Hermon Cawthra (1886-1971), a West Riding Art (Craft) Scholar from 1907-9, went on to the RCA from 1909-11. In 1912 a figure composition he had completed in marble as a Leeds student was selected for the RA summer exhibition and he became an RA student from 1912-16. Cawthra was to sculpt the groups of putti flanking Vincent Harris's Civic Hall at Leeds in 1933. The School was also delighted to record that Philip Naviasky (1894-1983) followed him to the RA Schools in 1913. The son of Jewish refugees from Russia, he had come on a Senior Scholarship in 1911 and was to return to spend most of his life in the area as a portrait painter.

The five years leading up and into the First World War were to provide the small 'art world' of Leeds with a dramatic exposure to new developments in European and British art. This was due to the arrival of two men, already of national significance, who searched out or founded associations that would fulfil their public-educational aims. The first was Michael Sadler (1861-1943), a pioneer of extra-mural education and the 1902 Education Act, who became Vice-Chancellor of Leeds University in 1911. A compulsive collector, he displayed his pictures at Buckingham House in Headingley Lane and, within the year, extended the first of several invitations to selected students and staff of the School to view them. He lent them watercolours and came to present the prizes.[37]

The second was Frank Rutter (1876-1937), the *Sunday Times* art critic who organised the Allied Artists' Association exhibitions at the Albert Hall as an English *Salon des Réfusés*. He coined the term Post-Impressionist and called for experimental art to be taken seriously. Attracted by Sadler's collection of works by Kandinsky and other Leeds acquisitions, he applied for the vacant curatorship of Leeds City Art Gallery in 1912. Finding no municipal purchasing fund, within a few months he and Sadler had launched the Leeds Art Collections Fund as a means of 'smuggling really good things into the gallery'. Haywood Rider and WH Thorp were founding members. For two years Rutter brought new types of art into the gallery – London Underground posters, Japanese woodcuts, paintings by Paul Nash, and the Pissarros. When most of the Gallery became the wartime Central Food Office, Rutter turned to other ways of developing an appreciation of contemporary art in Leeds.[38]

As President of the Leeds Arts Club, Rutter was able to invite leading artists to speak at the meetings which were often held in Sadler's house, and where Rutter's formalist approach to abstract modernism in art took issue with Sadler's more romantic expressionism. Walter Sickert (1860-1942) came to lecture and several recent graduates from the Slade in the Camden Town and London Groups were invited to Leeds in 1912-14 including Charles Ginner, Harold Gilman, Paul Nash and his brother John, and John Currie. In 1916 Sadler invited the Serbian refugee Ivan Mestrovic to lecture and Rutter arranged for an exhibition of his sculpture to come on from the V & A despite the city councillors' distaste for it.[39]

The Leeds Arts Club exhibitions and public lectures offered stimulating opportunities to students at the School of Art. Percy Teasdale, the School's specialist teacher of painting, was a regular attender and his work was shown and discussed at the Club. Sadler devoted considerable attention to young artists in Leeds, in particular Jacob Kramer and Bruce Turner of the School of Art and Herbert Read, a university student. TE Hulme's series of articles in *The New Age* introduced the work of Epstein and the London avant-garde to young artists like these. In May 1914, just before launching the Vorticist Movement, Wyndham Lewis(1882-1957) opened the Club's exhibition of Cubist and Vorticist Art.[40]

Bruce Turner (c1894-1962) responded with vigour. In 1911, just after leaving the School, he met Tom Heron who introduced him to the Arts Club circle and those who gathered around Alfred Orage in London, where Turner may have spent a brief period at the RCA. One member, the Spanish university lecturer Dr Penzol, introduced Turner to the work of Juan Gris and other Cubists, while the influence of Post-Impressionism can be seen in the bold colours and expressive brushwork of his portrait of Heron c1916 in the collections of Leeds City Art Gallery. Turner was a victim of the First World War. Unlike the Quaker, Ernest Procter, who immediately registered as a conscientious objector, and served from 1916 in the Friends Ambulance Unit becoming an Official War Artist just before the Armistice in 1918, Turner suffered the privations of imprisonment when he refused to take up arms and had a mental breakdown. When Tom Heron set up Cresta Silks Turner produced designs for him, but he never fully recovered and his work is too little known.[41]

On the eve of his enlistment in 1918, the Leeds Art Club mounted an exhibition of Kramer's work. By then he had joined Rutter's Allied Artists Association. But, unlike Mark Gertler (1891-1939) his near contemporary at the Slade, Kramer never fitted into the Bloomsbury Group or followed Roger Fry's interest in Cubism. Wyndham Lewis, who published a cartoon by Kramer in the second issue of *Blast* in 1915, took him up. But he was no Vorticist either. As Herbert Read (1893-1968), whom he met in 1912 and corresponded with during the war, aptly said, 'Kramer is and always has been an expressionist'.[43] This was what appealed to Sadler who saw artists as visionaries. Rider took a more sober view and wrote warning him, 'So many have ruined a good career by folly and loose living – I have a special right to say this, because you belong to us and I want in the future that we shall always as now be proud of you.'[44]

Jacob Kramer (1892-1962) attended the School, which for twenty-seven years carried his name. The son of a Ukrainian Jewish refugee artist, he started evening classes in 1907 where Rider encouraged his talents. From 1909 he had a grant from the Jewish Education Aid Society and from 1910 a small job as caretaker of the School's art materials. He was permitted to retain his Senior Art Scholarship, awarded in 1911, despite censure for his erratic behaviour. Sadler bought Kramer's pictures and recommended them to *Colour* magazine, advanced him money and found him a place at the Slade in 1913. His work was immediately exhibited with the new groups in London and Rutter publicly praised *Death of my Father* in 1916 when it was included in Kramer's joint exhibition with Fred Lawson at the Leeds School that November. Sadler felt moved to say that:

He had interpreted to them the humanity, the romance and pathos of the life of their city. There lay behind some of the drawings an intensity of family feeling, and a recollection of old far-off unhappy things, which gave to the work a depth of meaning which more and more appealed to them as they knew the drawings well.[42]

In 1915, as male students left to join up and boys ceased to enter from the schools, the War affected the School with increasing severity despite the recognition of its architecture and teacher training courses. The National Competition was still maintained and Leeds introduced etching in 1916, taking Frank Short's department at the RCA as a model. But by then enrolments had fallen to 230, mostly evening students and women, and only half the number of local scholarships were being awarded. Several of the craftwork courses ceased to be viable so their special teachers were not re-engaged. Silas Paul, the wrought-ironwork teacher resigned in 1915, probably for war work. With the introduction of conscription in 1916 the Head of Architecture was 'called to the colours' and replaced by a temporary appointment. Charles Broughton registered as a conscientious objector, but when the School asked for Broughton to continue his evening course in modelling doll's heads, a wartime venture into toy-making now the German sources were closed, the City Council refused. So the Modelling Department was closed.

The lowest notes were struck during the winter of 1916-17 when a student wrote 'expressing the desire of the students that no prizes should be offered this year.'[45] A Sub-Committee member offered a small prize for a Village Memorial Cross design. Only seventeen entered for the Board of Education and five for the City and Guilds exams. Student numbers fell to 133. Perhaps to counter this, the City's Education Department had published a substantial development plan in 1915, which included the potential recognition of the School as a 'College of Art' for advanced work, but it was shelved until after the war. That October the National Competition was cancelled and the Board of Education began to rearrange and simplify the exam system. There was a crisis in awarding local scholarships because the Board of Education did not accept the standard of selected candidates.

By the end of 1917, morale must have improved. The Phil May Memorial Committee endowed a Phil May Prize for the best drawings produced by students at the School each year. The first award, in 1918, and the Village War Memorial prize were won by future RCA scholars. And the students put on a dramatic sketch with a sale of work to buy Christmas presents for students of the School on active service. Thorp took over the chair from Kitson and maintained the momentum of the Architecture Department by enlisting the support of Professor Abercrombie of Liverpool University for a post-war course on Design as applied to Town Planning. Raymond Unwin's and Abercrombie's public course of lectures re-launched the School in its first full year of peace in 1919.

At the end of 1918 only five students passed the Board of Education exams in Drawing, two in Pictorial Design, and one in Industrial Design – a far cry from the pre-war records. Rider began the School's revival by enlisting his craftwork contacts to put on courses for disabled ex-servicemen. Alderman Leigh offered a prize for designs 'to commemorate peace' and there was an influx of books from parents whose architecture-student sons had been killed in the war.

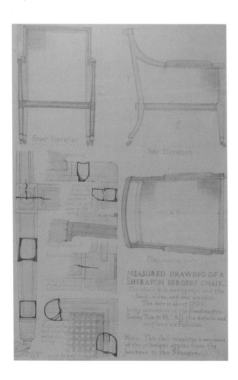

T: Memorial to Men of Leeds
...ucation Services by The Abbott,
Simpson and L Rogers, 1922
...ass, glass and enamel
y of Leeds Benefits Office,
...eat George Street

...ght: Measured Drawing of a
...eraton Bergere Chair c1790 in
...e Possession of the Headmaster
Alan W Bellis, c1904-5
...ncil and watercolour
...x 45.5 cm
...ivate Collection

Enrolments increased fast, almost reaching pre-war levels in 1919-20 with 400 (111 Day, 302 Evening, and 77 Day and Evening) students. These included men on ex-servicemen's training grants like Raymond Coxon (1896-1997) and Henry Moore (1898-1986). In February 1919 the School's Sub-Committee called for the Modelling Department to be reopened as soon as possible and in March, armed with a letter from the students, they urged the reinstatement of Charles Broughton as Head of the Modelling Department. Those who had left to fight had their jobs to return to, but the City Councillors continued to veto the rights of conscientious objectors. Walter Marsden MC ARCA withdrew his application and it was not until January 1920 that Reginald Cotterill ARCA, on the recommendation of the RCA Principal, could take up the post.[46] The revived significance of Modelling was emphasised by co-opting Caldwell Spruce onto the School's Sub-Committee for what were to be the last two years of his life.

Moore has given the impression that he was virtually the only Modelling student and rather overburdened by Cotterill's tuition. But there were other students who did not intend to specialise in the subject like Coxon, and some who did like Jocelyn Horner (1902-73). Moore's sketchbook indicates the importance of Architectural Ornament in the teaching, with allegorical subjects typical of the 'New Sculpture', and his lecture notes are devoted to classical sculpture. But his student works, which Jocelyn Horner bequeathed to the City Art Gallery, suggest that Moore was already looking elsewhere for ideas such as Sadler's collection before he found the London Museums. In 1920 Barbara Hepworth (1903-75) joined the School and, after a year studying drawing, accompanied Moore, Coxon and Edna Ginesi to 'the Leeds table' at the RCA in 1921.[47]

The year before they left, the RCA's new Principal, William Rothenstein (1878-1945), a painter trained at the Slade and the Académie Julian was involved in a major Leeds project. During the war, as Professor of Civic Art at Sheffield in 1916 he had advocated the role of Town Halls in public patronage: 'The Town Hall should be the symbolic centre of the life and creative industry of the whole neighbourhood; each succeeding year should add something to its completeness'.[48]

Sadler took this up on his return from India and in 1920 he proposed a mural scheme for the bare walls of Brodrick's Town Hall. It provided an opportunity for the young artists trained in London to demonstrate their skills under Rothenstein's supervision. Most of the seven artists came from Yorkshire or had brought their work to Leeds before the war. Jowett had studied at the School and so had Kramer, back in the city after several acclaimed exhibitions of his work. Two of his paintings had been presented to Leeds City Art Gallery by the Leeds Jewish Community in 1920. The School's architecture students contributed measured drawings of the wall spaces for the project. But when the *Yorkshire Post* published the sketches the response was abusive. Mark Senior (1864-1927), the Yorkshire Impressionist and a founder member of the Leeds Arts Club, condemned 'these artistic bolsheviks' and their 'nightmare crudities' while Kramer, who had recently publicly criticised the City Council for not using their gallery to display Sadler's and Rider's fine private collections, replied in their defence. Rothenstein also spoke up for his 'brilliant group of young men. . . who only await the encouragement that ought to be forthcoming from our great religions and municipal bodies.'[49] But without City Council approval there would be no donations. Sadler was forced to call it off admitting 'the designs, taken as a group are discordant with one another and would not be suitable for collective decoration.'[50] There would be no municipal Modernism.

Sadler had one more project, which was dedicated just before he left to become Master of University College, Oxford in 1923, the Leeds University War Memorial. Sculpted directly in stone by Eric Gill (1882-1942), a central figure of the Arts and Crafts Movement as it had developed on the Guild Socialist lines advocated by the Leeds Art Club founders. It is instructive to compare this with the memorial made by the design staff of the School of Art to commemorate their colleagues in the Leeds Educational Services who fell 1914-18. Sadler was impressed by Gill's unexecuted project for a war memorial subject of *Christ Driving the Money Changers Out of the Temple* and when he received a legacy in 1917 for his work at the university he commissioned this design. But the finished work was radically different because Gill used contemporary dress to condemn fashionable ladies, businessmen and money lenders. The Leeds press was outraged but Sadler praised it despite his embarrassment by a pamphlet

Gill published.[51] So did Rothenstein who referred to it when he opened the new academic year at the School in 1923, as an 'example of the true in art. . . one of the greatest pieces of sculpture in the last hundred years' and proceeded to encourage people 'to take themselves to their neighbour-craftsman and make him give them what they themselves wanted' rather than filling their houses with Chippendale and Sheraton furniture. He also congratulated Leeds on providing 'some of the most vital men at the Royal College. He only wished that they showed a greater tendency to return.'[52]

Only a few months before the University Memorial, another had been unveiled at the Town Hall to the men of the Leeds Education Services who fell in the same war. It may now be seen in the stair hall of the City of Leeds Benefits Office at Great George Street. It takes the form of a brass tablet with the forty-four names in repoussé, flanked by panels of green opalescent glass with bell-shaped swags. The civic coat of arms is placed above a red and white enamelled cross of sacrifice with the words *'Dulce et Decorum'* below. It was designed by Captain THE Abbott, back from the war, HE Simpson and Leonard Rogers of the School of Art.[53] If Sadler's commission expresses his originality and one direction for future British sculpture, this represents the sort of excellence in design craftsmanship that Rider had spent his career developing at the School. It remained for Barbara Hepworth and Henry Moore, with Herbert Read's critical support, to develop a quite different form of

Modernism from either of these products of the Arts and Crafts Movement.

Rider had in fact retired that summer, to eloquent tributes. By then there were 159 full-time students at the School, 41 of them ex-servicemen, and 444 attending part-time in the day and evening. The recent RCA results now showed that the majority of students there from Leeds were students of Painting with three in Sculpture and one in Design. But the Board of Education inspectors:

characterise the School as being well-staffed, and speak highly of the work done both in the direction of fine and applied Art. The headmaster. . . who during thirty-three years of office has been largely responsible for the development of the School from a school of drawing, painting and paper design to one in which the practical application of Art to Industry is a predominant feature, retired at the end of the year.[54]

Rider's successor was Harold H Holden, ARCA (1885-1977). He was one of his pre-war students, who had come back to the School staff to teach art at the adjacent Boys' Modern School in 1910, and headed Cheltenham School of Art from 1914.

Evolving Forms

From Mobelling to Carving

Matthew Withey

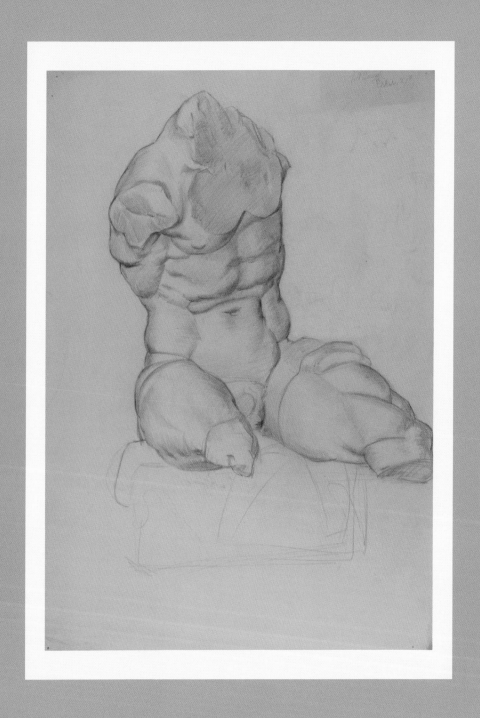

EVOLVING FORMS
FROM MODELLING TO CARVING IN THE SCULPTURE DEPARTMENT 1919-39

MATTHEW WITHEY

The two most celebrated artists ever to pass through the doors of the Vernon Street building were both sculptors. Henry Moore enrolled at the school in 1919 and crammed Walter Buckley Pearson's two-year drawing course into his first year, then specialised in sculpture with Reginald Cotterill for his second. He secured a scholarship to study at the Royal College of Art in London in 1921. Barbara Hepworth arrived in Leeds one year after Moore and joined him at the Royal College of Art in 1921, having also completed the drawing course in one year. Both artists went on to become key contributors to twentieth century sculpture in Britain and abroad, and the fact that they emerged at the same time, from the same regional art school, does tend to focus one's attention on the whys and wherefores of how sculpture was taught in Leeds during and after their time there. For this reason, the following essay will concentrate on the School of Sculpture and Modelling in the two decades subsequent to 1919.

Talented sculptors, most notably Hermon Cawthra and the medallist Percy Metcalfe, had come through before the First World War, when Sculpture and Modelling was headed by Edward Caldwell Spruce. But it was after Moore and Hepworth's spell there that Leeds came to be recognised as the important centre it is for the teaching and enjoyment of three-dimensional art. Cotterill, an associate of the Royal College of Art, was invited to re-establish the sculpture course in 1919, apparently in response to Moore's wish to take the Board of Education examination.[1] The time-honoured lines along which he set the curriculum are illustrated by a College prospectus from session 1923-4, in which Cotterill notes that the department's demonstration plaster casts:

. . .are from examples of the finest type of figure work and ornament, and have been collected with a view to furnishing representative examples of all the best periods of artistic work. These examples are used as a basis of study for the development of the design faculty, and as a guide in the manner of good taste and sound workmanship.[2]

Moore would have benefited from training in the modelling of natural objects such as leaves, birds and animals; historic examples of ornament; drapery; design – from elementary to designing for specific crafts; antique details and figures; anatomy; and life – details and figures. He would also have received instruction in the history of sculpture; architecture in relation to sculpture; and lettering – modelled and incised. His most recent biographer claims, however, that classes in wood and stone carving were not available,[3] which is surprising because Hepworth's biographer suggests these were up-and-running by 1920, though Hepworth herself elected not to study sculpture until enrolled at the Royal College of Art.[4] Tuition in wood and stone carving, metalwork and pottery was certainly available to Leeds College of Art students by 1923-4. It was taught once a week by a local craftsman named J Lawrance. Lawrance also ran evening classes in carving for part-time students wishing to take their City and Guilds exam.

Largely due to comments made by Moore himself, Cotterill's sculpture course has tended to be dismissed as formulaic and prescribed, usually by commentators with no particular understanding of the rigours of Board of Education assessment, or sympathy for the grounding to be gained from a solid programme of training in craft

LEFT: SHADED DRAWING OF THE BELVEDERE TORSO BY PAT BURRAS, 1937 PENCIL 55.8 X 38.1 CM LEEDS MUSEUMS AND GALLERIES (CITY ART GALLERY) © THE ARTIST DRAWING FROM PLASTER CASTS, BOTH FROM LIFE AND FROM MEMORY, WAS PART OF THE CURRICULUM FOR ALL STUDENTS TAKING THE DRAWING EXAM WHICH WOULD ALLOW THEM TO PROGRESS TO MORE SPECIALISED COURSES; FOR BURRAS THIS WAS PAINTING WHILE FOR MOORE IT WAS MODELLING.

RIGHT: SEATED NUDE MAN BY HENRY MOORE, c1920 PAINTED PLASTER 23 X 12 X 17.3 CM LEEDS MUSEUMS AND GALLERIES (CITY ART GALLERY) © THE HENRY MOORE FOUNDATION

technique.[5] For those who wanted it, access to the more modish branches of contemporary sculpture was available via the departmental library, which Cotterill described in the 1923-4 prospectus as 'well equipped with works of the best and most up-to-date description'. These might have included monographic volumes on the sculpture of Alexander Archipenko, Jacob Epstein, Adolf von Hildebrand, George Kolbe, Wilhelm Lehmbruck, Ivan Mestrovic and Auguste Rodin, all of which were published in the years between 1919 and 1923, as were numerous pamphlets by Eric Gill and the St Dominic's Press at Ditchling. Contemporary survey books included two volumes of Kineton Parkes' *Sculpture of Today* (1921), *Modern British Sculpture* (1922), published by the Royal Society of British Sculptors with a foreword by AL Baldry, and *Niederlandische Plastik der Gegenwart* (1922), a book of contemporary Dutch sculpture with illustrations of fascinating Art Deco and early modernist works by the likes of HF Bieling, Barend Jordens and Thomas André Vos. Students may also have had access to some of the modernist art theory books doing the rounds at this time, for instance *Vision and Design* (1920) by Roger Fry, *The New Art* (1922) by Horace Shipp and *Since Cezanne* by Clive Bell (1922).

Most guidance, though, would have come directly from the head of the department. Cotterill oversaw all the modelling classes, including three Wednesday sessions (morning, afternoon, evening) in modelling from life. In many ways, 1923-4 was a good year for Leeds. There were 892 students enrolled at the school, an increase of 178 on the previous year.[6] Of these, four students managed to secure scholarships to the Royal College of Art, and twenty-eight passed the Board of Education examinations for 1924: six in drawing, three in painting and eighteen in the two grades of industrial design. Just one of the passes was in modelling, which gives us some idea of how few students chose to specialise in sculpture at this time, even with the mounting accomplishments of Henry Moore as a spur.[7] The most noteworthy undergraduate of the period was probably Mrs Ethel Cotterill (née Goldberg), the sculpture master's young wife. In November 1924, aged twenty-two, she won the British Institute's Scholarship in Sculpture, an award worth £150.[8] Her prize-winning design – an elegant but chastely classical fountain – demonstrates perfectly the established criteria for judging sculpture in 1920s Britain, and rather contradicts the post-Herbert Read orthodoxy which says that the interwar years were a ferment of modernist rebellion. Although clearly the work of a naturally gifted artist, it also illustrates RT Cotterill's proficiency in drumming good practice into his students, especially in the modelling of classical ornament and figures. One of his last students at Leeds, Jocelyn Horner, confirmed this with a lifetime of refined figure work.[9]

LEFT: PAGE FROM THE LEEDS SCHOOL OF ART SKETCHBOOK OF HENRY MOORE, 1919, SHOWING A SKETCH AFTER MESTROVIC
LEEDS MUSEUMS AND GALLERIES (CITY ART GALLERY)
© THE HENRY MOORE FOUNDATION

ABOVE: BARBARA HEPWORTH AGED 18 AT THE ROYAL COLLEGE OF ART, LONDON, 1921
COURTESY OF ALAN BOWNESS

In 1927, while still studying under Cotterill, Horner's bronze statuette *Realisation* was exhibited at the Royal Academy.[10] By this time, AE Warnes had replaced J Lawrance as wood carving instructor and R Longbottom had been taken on as the assistant responsible for marble and stone carving.[11]

The basic layout of the sculpture course at Leeds College of Art remained in place even after Cotterill left to become principal of York School of Arts and Crafts.[12] His replacement, the twenty-three-year-old Scotsman Loris Hector Rey, arrived in Leeds in December 1927, soon after the opening of the annual Leeds College of Art exhibition.[13] Such was the scale of Rey's impact on teaching methods at Leeds, and such is the lack of attention generally given to his career, that a brief biographical digression is warranted. He was born in Rutherglen on 11 December 1903, the elder son of a French father and Scottish mother. Writing in 1933, John Rothenstein, then curator of Leeds City Art Gallery, noted that Rey's paternal grandfather was one of the printers of the seditious leaflets with which Victor Hugo attacked the government of Napoleon III, and he shared with the poet the exile that his republican activities were liable to bring.[14]

Rey's education began at St Aloysius school in Glasgow and continued for a brief spell at St Phillip's Grammar School in Birmingham. Back in Glasgow, he decided on a career as a chemist and took a job in a chemical factory near the city, attending night classes at the West of Scotland Technical College in an effort to secure his BSc. A sudden slump in the chemical market led to his redundancy, however, and after thirteen weeks of unemployment, Rey was taken on – at the age of seventeen – as an apprentice of William Vickers, a moderately successful stone carver and architectural sculptor. Given Rey's schooling, it is interesting to note that Vickers sculpted the high altar at St Aloysius Church between 1908 and 1910. He also taught design, decorative art and stone carving at Glasgow School of Art from around 1898 until 1920. Vickers would have made an able mentor for his young assistant, but his sudden death in 1922 left Rey with no option but to partner his employer's widow in the running of the family business. This arrangement abided for the better part of a year, before Rey entered Glasgow School of Art, where Vickers' post in the Sculpture Department had been taken over by Archibald Dawson.

The head of the Sculpture Department at this time was Alexander Proudfoot, a collaborator with Dawson and Benno Schotz on the superb scheme of Art Deco sculpture at Glasgow's Mercat Cross building, completed in 1928. Dawson would go on, in the 1930s, to contribute carved decoration to at least two of Gillespie, Kidd and Coia's famous cycle of modernist Roman Catholic churches, an interesting point given that Rey himself was a Catholic, working in a field where freemasonry was commonplace, and living in Glasgow at a time when sectarian divisions were profound. In the meantime, though, Rey's teacher

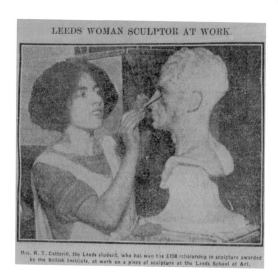

LEEDS WOMAN SCULPTOR AT WORK.

Mrs. E. T. Cotterill, the Leeds student, who has won the £150 scholarship in sculpture awarded by the British Institute, at work on a piece of sculpture at the Leeds School of Art.

was producing exquisite Art Deco sculpture for buildings such as EG Wylie's American classical-style offices for the Scottish Legal Assurance Society (1927-31) and the headquarters of North British and Mercantile (1926-9), Sir JJ Burnet's last commission in his home city.

Rey gained his diploma in 1926 and was awarded the Keppie and Haldane Travelling Scholarship the same year. Versions of this award had been won in the past by both Vickers and Proudfoot, and it enabled Rey to familiarise himself for the first time with continental sculpture. On his return to Glasgow he took up a part-time teaching appointment at the art school. Rey later destroyed his work from this period, and his apprentice work with William Vickers Ltd has proved impossible to trace. In December 1927, however, despite any uncertainties we may have about the quality of his early work, he became Head of the School of Sculpture and Modelling at Leeds College of Art, following a glowing recommendation from Proudfoot. His studio in Leeds was at 48a Back Cowper Street – the same studio, coincidentally, as used earlier by Edward Caldwell Spruce, one of Rey's predecessors

YOUNG SCULPTOR'S APPOINTMENT.— Mr. Loris H. Rey, who has been appointed head of the sculpture department of Leeds College of Art, is only 24 years old.

in the Sculpture Department. Rothenstein reports that the new sculpture master was ignorant of Frank Dobson and Jacob Epstein until at least 1926. 'Instead of such men as these he took for his models the Romanesque and Gothic sculptors, whose work he had studied on his travels, those of Northern France especially.' Not until he came to Leeds did Rey familiarise himself with the 'contemporary spirit'.

In or around 1934, shortly after resigning from his post in the sculpture department, Rey moved first to Bridge of Weir near Glasgow, then to London. Working out of various small studios in Chelsea, his career from this point, if not spectacular, was certainly interesting and productive, and reflected contemporary thought on the representation of the head and figure as advanced by such respected practitioners as Eric Gill, Epstein, Dobson and Moore. His largest commission seems to have come via a body called the Catholic Guild of Artist-Craftsmen and consisted of the designs for panels of the Stations of the Cross for a small church in Spain. Unfortunately, the outbreak of the Spanish Civil War in 1936 put an end to this assignment, and Rey's designs exist only as charcoal works on paper.[15]

Rey's first and only solo exhibition, in early 1939 at the Matthieson's Gallery on New Bond Street in London, was tepidly received by the press. TW Earp asserted that 'his danger, in an art often confined to a cramped imitation of reality, is too great a fluency. . . [however] when the sculptural sense is free and unshadowed by influences, as with the charming "Fountain Head", a striking plastic impulse is asserted'.[16] Rey showed regularly at the Royal Academy from around the time of his first solo exhibition, with portraiture and religious work accounting for most of his practice. Among others, the war years saw him producing busts of the civil servant and linguist Sir Ernest Gowers and the theatre impresario Sir Bronson Albery, while also serving as a volunteer in the Auxiliary Fire Service; Rey actually appeared in *Fires Were Started*, Humphrey Jennings' 1943 documentary tribute to the firefighters of London. He also designed a Trinity figure for the Christ Church Gateway in Canterbury. After the war, his career as a sculptor faded gradually, though he did continue exhibiting at the Royal Academy until 1953. Rey was also an energetic member of the Chelsea Arts Club. 'An extremely likeable man who

LEFT: LORIS REY SOON AFTER HIS ARRIVAL IN LEEDS
DAILY SKETCH 6 DECEMBER 1927
LEEDS SCHOOL OF ART
PRESS CUTTING ALBUM
LEEDS METROPOLITAN UNIVERSIT

gathered friends around him like moths round a bright light', he died on 17 August 1962, succumbing to a cancer of the pancreas.[17]

Perhaps because of his young age when he arrived in Leeds, Rey's approach to teaching was less rigid than Cotterill's, and though the curriculum remained the same at first, the ethos of the department quickly changed. By late 1929, Douglas Andrews, the Principal of Leeds College of Art, was able to point out that 'we try to imbue the students with a sense of sculptural form rather than to induce them to make life-like reproductions'.[18] Sculpture figured prominently in that year's annual College exhibition at Leeds City Art Gallery, with Thomas Allen, Maxwell Davidson and C Harrison eliciting particular praise, though a contemporary description of their work suggests that a no-nonsense, traditional approach to passing the Board of Education examinations was still at the heart of how students were taught.[19] Nevertheless, one commentator was prompted to gush that:

this [the sculpture] department of the College of Art seems to progress by leaps and bounds. The exhibits indicate a tendency to encourage self-expression in the students rather than academic discipline, and this policy has achieved some very happy results.[20]

Hubert Hatcher, a student noted for his command of the figure, passed the Board of Education examination for modelling in 1931, and although this type of sculpture remained as the course's basic rule of thumb, animalia and stone carving were becoming more popular with students. A ram's head, probably by Thomas Allen and sculpted from a block of stone rescued from demolished buildings on De Grey Terrace, Leeds, was one of the key exhibits at the annual show of 1930, held again at Leeds City Art Gallery.[21] The following year, Maxwell Davidson exhibited another of his lions' heads, prompting pictures in both the *Leeds Mercury* and the *Yorkshire Evening Post*.[22] And in 1932, Rothenstein purchased Allen's sculpture of *The Bull* for Leeds City Art Gallery, the work having been carved directly in Portland stone a year

earlier, without the aid of drawings or models.[23] Despite his skills with the chisel, Allen passed his Board of Education examination in modelling in 1933.[24] Direct carving was still relatively new to the sculpture department in Leeds. Nevertheless, Rey's tenure was marked by an eagerness to encourage an intuitive style of carving, and he can also be credited with introducing such novel materials as lead and artificial stone to his lessons on casting.[25] This willingness to bring fresh approaches to tried-and-tested teaching methods tallies with the friendships Rey struck with Jacob Kramer and Sir Michael Sadler, great advocates of modernist art, and Leeds' outstanding cultural figures in the 1920s and 30s.[26] It is also borne out by his introduction to the sculpture course in the Leeds College of Art prospectus for the school year 1932-3. Updating this for the first time since Cotterill left, Rey notes that:

the work in the school cultivates the sense for artistic quality and encourages the realisation of individual character in students, and is distinctly useful to those who seek to understand the essential properties of creative art. At the same time, courses are arranged to suit all types of students and special instruction is given in all branches of decorative work that may give scope for modelling and carving.[27]

Rey resigned within a year of writing these words, but they remained as the Sculpture Department's mission statement even after he was replaced, in November 1933, by John Kavanagh.[28] Despite his accomplishments as a sculptor, Kavanagh appears to have been less successful as a teacher. His time in Leeds was marked, apparently, by just one pass in the Board of Education examination for modelling: Doreen Findlay in 1936.[29] However, he did manage to develop his own practice. In 1935, for instance, he won a bronze medal from the Societé des Artistes Françaises at the Grand Palais in Paris for his bronze sculpture *Wanda Tiburzzi*.[30] The following year, a bronze figure by Kavanagh, was presented to Roundhay Girls' High School by Miss MC Vyvyan, founder and former headmistress of the school.[31] And in 1938 he secured the commission to execute sculpture for Walthamstow Town Hall in London. It was in order to devote more time to this last job that Kavanagh left his post in January 1939.[32] He was replaced two months later by Douglas Bissett, another graduate of Glasgow School of Art.[33]

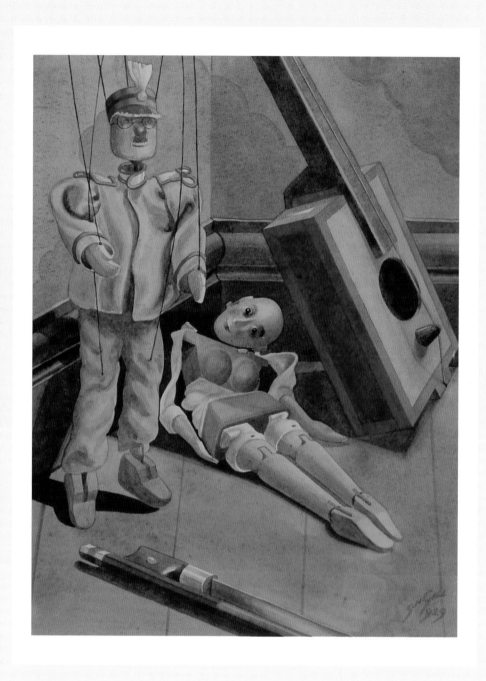

You had to attend regularly and punctually both day and evening, and Saturday morning classes, the timetable was mapped out for you and it was only late in student life you had much say in what you wanted to do. . . I soon became used to the long working hours in the city and enjoyed every class I attended, even measured drawing.

The first year course consisted of plant drawing, painting groups of objects in tone and others in watercolour and various exercises in the making of patterns called, strangely enough, abstract design. Afternoons were given over to craftwork like jewellery, silversmithing or leatherwork. It was a traditional training with the emphasis on technique rather than creativity.

After one term I, along with a male student, was promoted. This was a great 'leg up' and we were both allowed to enter that holy of holies the life class. It was fair treatment, one boy, one girl. After this initiation, drawing the human figure in the life class really took over, leading to an examination in drawing and followed by one in painting some years later. Both exams were very set, particularly the first, comprising as it did drawing from life, drawing from the cast (Venus de Milo, Discobolus, Belvedere Torso etc), Anatomy, Perspective and Memory Drawing. It was discipline – one sat on a 'donkey' or stood at an easel and learnt (by dint of observation and correction) to draw. My first half term was spent drawing a man holding a pole; it was really the painting student's pose; a monstrous exercise about which I never complained.

For the Painting Exam one was required to do a life canvas (set size, set pose), a still-life, a design, and a cartoon for a mural, as well as written texts on the history and methods of painting. The approach to the work was traditional. You learnt to use your eyes and develop what skills you had.

Amongst those I best remember, and to whom I am most indebted, was Percy Talbot of the Painting School. He taught both drawing and painting and although he was not officially responsible for the theoretical side. . . his knowledge of these things was wide and profound. He was an intellectual and loved discussion.

Despite the constraints imposed by the examination system, he encouraged us to think for ourselves, and try out new ideas, even though they might run counter to what was acceptable at the time. . . E Owen Jennings was a fine artist himself specialising in etching and engraving. . . He was a great teacher who never got ruffled. He just about had us eating out of his hand. . . Loris Rey from Glasgow who came to take charge of the sculpture – half French, half Scottish (a formidable mix). . . He was temperamental, excitable, quixotic and extremely gifted. . . On account of his charisma he soon became part of the art scene of Leeds itself. He came to know Jacob Kramer and my first sight of the latter was when I came across him sitting like a monolith to have his portrait sculpted.

It was not generally known, but Kramer came often into the School. One might be in the top sculpture studio of an evening when, to the accompaniment of crashing and falling screens, Jacob would emerge. He had come in the back way, the better, he said, to avoid being seen. He had made his way up the back stairs to come out at the top near the hoist. He invariably adopted this cloak and dagger approach by saying he was not welcome in the College – what rubbish!

A marked but tangible difference between the working conditions of yesterday's and today's students. . . is the light. Before the Smoke Abatement Act the industrial cities could become gloomy places to work in, particularly in winter. I recollect one day, when dark green smog enveloped everything, all the city lights came on at midday. In winter, to combat the darkness of the short northern days, we would commence the afternoon session at 1.30 and knock off at 3.30.

KATHERINE FRYER
JUNE 1994
LEEDS COLLEGE OF ART STUDENT 1926-32

LEFT: STILL-LIFE COMPOSITION
WITH PUPPETS BY SN GILL, 1929
PENCIL AND WATERCOLOUR
34.2 X 26 CM
PRIVATE COLLECTION

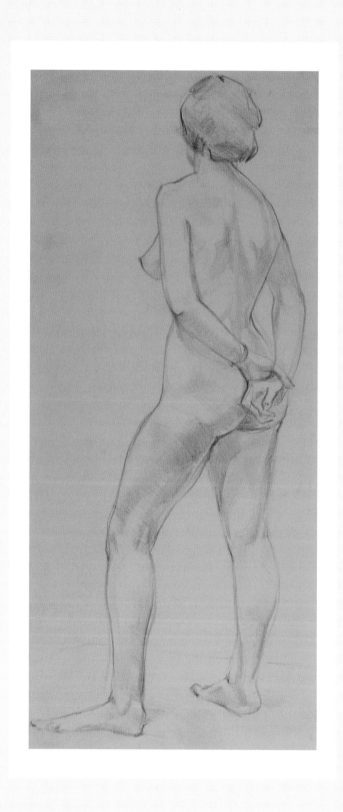

On entering the College the office was on the left. There Miss Wood and Miss White, two stern looking ladies in green overalls, seemed always to be watching students as they signed-in on a book that was kept on a shelf below a glass partition of the office. So it was difficult to arrive late or leave early without being noticed.

Behind the office was Room 10, the only room in the building to look like a school classroom. . . Outside No.10 the walls were covered with students' lockers, tall enough to take a half-imperial drawing board. . . There were steps down to the basement [to] the girls' common room, a gloomy place with one window so high that the only things visible through it were the feet and legs of passersby on the pavement of the street outside.

. . . in the entrance hall was a plaster cast of Winged Victory.

One of the female nude models called Della Questa had posed for several famous artists when she was younger. Another model was an attractive Spanish girl. Her husband was also a model at the College.

As well as day lessons most students went to night school three or four nights a week. Those students who lived out of Leeds passed the time between day and evening sessions by visiting the Art Gallery or the Library, or just walking around the back alleyways where the Merrion Centre is now. The things in the City Art Gallery that impressed me most during that time were Sickert's Juliet and the Nurse, Orpen and Brangwyn's work, Butler's Political Prisoner and the drawings for Picasso's Guernica.

I was given 1/3d per day and, with that, I could get a three-course meal at Lewis's or other department stores, or Woolworths.

One student came to College dressed all in black leather with heavy knee-length boots and carried a black leather cushion, which seemed a strange thing for such a menacing looking youth to carry everywhere. He said it was because he had piles. He had been arrested for causing trouble at Oswald Mosley's rallies in Leeds. Instead of sending him to borstal he was given the chance to learn a trade and chose to come to the Art College in order to learn signwriting. This he found very useful; there were no paints in aerosol cans at that time, so he got to know the easiest and quickest way to paint fascist slogans on walls.

Painting Examination – the College provided stretchers of the size necessary for the Exam. The students had to buy canvas or hessian and stretch it and prime it with whiting mixed with size. One painting to be sent to the Examiners had to be of a figure composition. The students could choose whatever subject they wished and paint it at any time before the Exam. For the still-life a list of objects was given to the students a few days before the Exam. These had to be brought to College; each student set up his own group and painted it in a given time. The nude model was posed according to instructions from the examiners. The students had no choice as to where they painted, positions were allocated to them. There was also a written paper on the History of Art in Europe and on Methods of Painting.

There was a busy social side to College. . . Every Friday between day school and night school there was a 'Hop' in Room 10. Entrance was 2d. The money was used to buy records, until later some of the boys formed a band . . . There was a Freshers dance at the Tea Rooms in the Headrow and a dinner dance at the Victory Hotel in Briggate. This was not a success as not many of the students had evening dress. So after that, they had fancy dress dances.

MAISIE SMITH (NÉE BROWNFOOT)
MARCH 1992
LEEDS COLLEGE OF ART STUDENT 1935-40

LEFT: LIFE STUDY
BY MAISIE SMITH c1937
PENCIL 34.5 X 15 CM
PRIVATE COLLECTION

THE LEEDS EXPERIMENT
THE STORY OF A NEW CREATIVITY

INÉS PLANT

LEEDS
COLLEGE
OF ART

OPEN
WEEK

13-18 OCTOBER

11 am - 7.30 pm

THE LEEDS EXPERIMENT
THE STORY OF A NEW CREATIVITY

In 1945, the man who became known as the heavyweight champion of art and design education, Edward E Pullée, was appointed Principal of Leeds College of Art. Pullée found Vernon Street run more like a school than a college. To the students, wearing the smart maroon and beige striped blazer and college scarf, the staff could seem remote and majestic figures. On 8 February every year there was a one-day holiday to celebrate the birthday of John Ruskin the influential Victorian art writer, painter, and promoter of the Arts and Crafts movement.

After the Second World War, a greater diversity of ages, backgrounds and aspirations became apparent in the student profile of the Leeds College of Art. There were ex-servicemen and women, scholarship pupils, some who paid their way with part-time jobs, and students straight from school; all had to make their way through a formal and hierarchical system. The College training was still academic, and drawing skills were the starting point for both craft and fine art courses, as they had been throughout the previous century. Throughout the war, despite difficulties with supplies of paper and other art materials, the high standards set for drawing skills were maintained.

Post-war, at first, things carried on as before but the 1950s saw an easing of post-war sobriety; a lighter side to College life was beginning to emerge. The Annual Arts Ball was a much-loved event, and Leeds College of Art had its own jazz band, The Vernon Street Ramblers, which was much in demand especially during Rag Week.

Even before his appointment to Leeds, Edward Pullée felt that education 'had already started to change. It had opened out.'[1] He had heard about some innovative art teaching taking place in North Yorkshire, and came to know Harry Thubron. This led to Vernon Street, becoming the site for an experimental approach to creativity. Thus when Edward Pullée decided to appoint Thubron as Head of Painting in 1955, it was a deliberate choice for change.

Laurie Burt recalled:

Young, inspired, open-minded lecturers were appointed, and practising artists. . . brought in to teach part-time. . . This fresh impetus in Leeds College – of teaching ideas more 'art now'. . . was due to the evangelistic fervour of an artist and lecturer called Harry Thubron. . . Almost overnight, previously uneventful college days became times of intense, unending excitement. Art became a great adventure – a voyage of discovery into previously unconsidered uses of materials and daring new ways of painting and making, of shaping and constructing.[2]

Harry Thubron trained at Sunderland School of Art and then spent two years at the Royal College of Art in London. During his five years in the Army, from 1940, he set up schools for Army personnel. Thubron had no formal teacher training, but in the Army he learnt to 'communicate', and to engage the interest of diverse groups of people. After the war Thubron taught fine art – first at West Hartlepool, then at Sunderland College of Art. It was while he was teaching at the latter that Maurice de Sausmarez introduced him to John Wood, the Art, Music and Drama Advisor for the North Riding Education Authority. John Wood's summer schools in Scarborough, though targeted primarily at local schoolteachers, were open to the general public. Thubron was invited to teach, and was subsequently asked to head a four-month experimental course for the North Riding Education Authority, at the Joseph Rowntree Secondary School in New Earswick. John Wood moved to the Leeds Education Authority in 1957, where he became a valuable ally in his support of the College of Art.

ABOVE: LETTER FROM HARRY THUBRON
1955
COURTESY OF NATIONAL ARTS
EDUCATION ARCHIVE, BRETTON HALL
© ELMA THUBRON

Thubron's appearance in Vernon Street is said to have electrified both staff and students immediately. How did the introduction of one new member of staff impact on a school of art which already enjoyed a reputation for excellence? It was not just personality but a dramatic change to the physical space in which he worked. On the back of a typewritten essay, Thubron wrote: 'I arranged with Edward Pullée to remove the partition in the large room in the old college. He gave me what he called his dozen best students and this new space.'[3] The previous two studios on the top floor, now one, could accommodate eighty or more students, and after quite a short time, did so.

After the carpentry work, Thubron collected together his 'Instructors'. Thubron chose not to plough a lone furrow when teaching. Some years later he wrote to Victor Pasmore: 'the difference between you and I was that I designed teams.'[4] A student of 1961 to 1962 recollected the teaching at the College as 'a team effort. But the spirit of it was Thubron' and as the years passed 'most of the people that were employed on it were ex-students of Thubron's'.[5] Some of the outstanding, and earliest recruits to Thubron's teaching team were Tom Watt, Gavin Stewart and Eric (Ricky) Atkinson. Tom Hudson, also Head of Evening School, joined the team as teacher in Painting Methods.

No time was wasted, and the 'dozen best students' were given individual projects to tackle. For one exercise they were each given a block of alabaster about ten centimetres square, and told to work slowly with hand tools, not to decide a pre-conceived shape, but to find in the stone a balance of planes over its three-dimensional form. They were told to work slowly. Each modification to the alabaster had to be an expression of an intuitive, sensitive response, seeing it as an organic, growing, shape. With fountain pen Thubron had added comments on the back of the typescript: 'The alabaster had two smooth and four rough sides – it was the way it was broken up!' Further notes explain that working on the outside of the form added to the inner form.[6]

Another exercise was to make a composition using two shapes with newsprint and charcoal. The shapes had to be dynamic, have tension and energy. Students were reminded that the three-dimensional alabaster forms were conceived as having centres from which a dynamic energy pushed out towards the surface. The relationship of the forms to one another was of prime importance – there had to be a feeling of tension between the shapes.

The principle, as with the alabaster exercise, was based on the model of 'organic' growth; on an analogy of a naturally-developing organism, the final shape of which was not predetermined by the student but arose slowly, intuitively, as the two forms grew side by side.[7]

Some of Harry Thubron's 'guinea pigs' got off to a slow start, unsure what they were supposed to be doing. Thubron had anticipated this, and the main task of the teams of roving instructors, was to talk to the students at work in the studios. Inevitably there were students who would try to impose a preconception, start to work to a plan, or were at a loss as to how to continue. The teachers encouraged students to clear their minds of possible influences, as previously accepted conventions could block out clear-sighted understanding of the task ahead. When asked to explain his teaching ideas, Thubron said: 'the actual Basic Training. . . is a balanced course involving disciplines and freedoms that are relative to the individual' and, no doubt equally perplexing to the newcomer, 'There are no answers other than those offered

by the student.'[8] It was the student's answer to the work in hand that had to be coaxed from him by the team of tutors in the studio. Students should achieve confidence in what they were doing by this method. Thubron was asking them to empty their minds of all previous ideas of what art was, or had been, or could be – especially the last, students must find their own forms of expression. Jon Thompson said Harry Thubron saw himself as enabler rather than teacher. Students were to use a 'spirit of exploration' as a tool to engage their potential. By describing himself as one of the 'great allowers' never as a pedant, Thompson says Thubron was arguing it was the teacher's job 'to set the scene but then not to direct the play'.[9] Students were encouraged to explore their sensibilities and learn to develop their work unselfconsciously. Thubron's wife, Elma Thubron, verified Thubron never countenanced any direct answers to people who wanted directions. 'By leaving them to work things out for themselves they dug deeper than they did before. They met parts of themselves they didn't know existed.'[10]

Harry Thubron had not under-estimated the disruption the new approach to teaching might entail in Vernon Street. Among his personal papers this statement was found:

The Leeds enterprise – virtually the total re-forming and re-structuring of a large college of art – was, on the face of it, a massive and immensely complicated task, requiring new theoretical stances, new organisational structures, new teaching strategies, new teacher/student relationships, new connections with the world of commerce and industry outside the school of art, new teacher to teacher relationships, and new connections with the educational authorities which controlled and governed the college.[11]

Many years later Edward Pullée reflected: 'Basic Design was never a structured, self-contained course, but a form of research and enquiry, an infection of people which came together organically and "grew like Topsy". It affected all courses'.[12] Thubron encouraged debate as a further aid to research. An outstanding recollection of those involved in the 'Leeds Enterprise' was the amount of discussion that took place – during the studio work, over a cup of tea, at the end of studio sessions, and at a small café across Vernon Street from the College (in a row of buildings long demolished). These endless discussions (as some remember them) seemed to be part of the new teaching strategy, removing any

LOW: LEFT TO RIGHT, TOMMY WATT, IC ATKINSON AND HARRY THUBRON, 57 COURTESY OF ERIC ATKINSON

barriers remaining between teachers and students. During an academic term, debate and discussion grew easier; students became more articulate and more confident.

Edward Pullée left one year after his appointment of Harry Thubron. Eric Taylor, then Head of the School of Design, became Principal of Leeds College of Art in 1956. Taylor was an artist and draughtsman of considerable ability. His thirteen years at Leeds College of Art were destined to be turbulent, but somehow he was able to keep any internecine disagreement in check. Taylor emphasised to his teaching staff that the interests of the students must come first. In the catalogue for an exhibition of student work Taylor wrote:

I believe that only by collective effort of the various specialists within a College can profound teaching be achieved, whether it be painting, sculpture or industrial design. . . The general education of the art student is a matter for much thought and there is no simple solution. We are attempting to avoid the falseness of superficial veneer by seeing the basic art training and the student's liberal education as one. . .[13]

It was agreed between Harry Thubron and Frank Chippendale, Head of the School, that students in their first year in the School of Architecture and Town Planning should take part in basic inter-disciplinary research. 'The new curriculum included figure drawing, still-life and painting as for fine art students.' Architectural students and students from the School of Drawing and Painting were given a joint project – to build a children's playground. As Brian Godward recalled, 'we found it difficult to work together with our different backgrounds. We were wanting to be specific and the artists were all wanting to explore shapes [though work continued for a week] we never did build it.' More successful was another project where students from Fine Art joined with students from Landscape in Architecture and the Building School. About this second project he was able to say, 'It was good for the way it creates a debate.'[14]

During the year students' work was project driven. The tasks set had to be accomplished within certain time limits. An entire week could be spent working with colour practice and theory. For other exercises, only black and white were allowed, but absolutely anything that was white or black; any base, medium and 'just anything that didn't actually move' could be used. It appeared there

was no pressure put on teaching staff or students, yet there was a sense of urgency and rapt concentration. Days would finish with a 'crit', a discussion, and sometimes a satisfying sense of achievement.

The Basic Research course appeared to be working well; it was organised to fit inside the College programmes and timetables. Favourable notices came from periodic inspections by the local authority. The City of Leeds Education Committee Annual Report 1957-1958 contained the following comment:

A significant development in art in the twentieth century has been the break from traditional methods, a concentration on imaginative power, rather than technical perfection. Artists have seen and proclaimed the limitations of the representational: they have come to feel that everything that can be done in the old way has already been done, and that they must find some new way of their own. Even if he accepts that his function is to portray the world he lives in, the modern artist lives in a fragmentary, hectic world.[15]

In 1958, despite this endorsement, the Board of Education examiners failed all those students entered for the Intermediate Examination from Leeds College of Art, in Vernon Street. Students previously buoyed up by their conviction of having the finest education imaginable must have been not only dismayed but also astonished. Examinations were set and marked by the Board of Education in South Kensington – as they had been before the College moved to Vernon Street in 1903 and students had to submit their portfolios, containing examples of the year's course work, to London for assessment.

It became essential for the teaching staff to reassess their attitude to the Kensington examination process. Irksome as the lack of autonomy was, the power of the national system had to be acknowledged. The teams were kept, but areas of responsibility were redefined. Instructors were allocated to ensure that every student prepared sufficient portfolio work of the sort preferred by the London examiners. The 1958 group re-sat the examinations and was successful. Of the previously failed Fine Art students, four went on to do Post-Graduate courses at the Slade School of Art, and won the three prestigious awards: the Prix de Rome, The Abbey Minor Scholarship and the Gulbenkian Scholarship. Thubron and the teams continued teaching students much as before, except that for a few

weeks every spring, more attention was paid to the Board of Education's formal requirements.

'In the late fifties and sixties the City's cultural vitality focused on art education and the pioneering experiments of Harry Thubron'.[16] It is only occasionally that circumstances and events come together in ways that reinforce and strengthen each other. In Leeds in the 1950s, in this unlikely black and sooty town, such events did take place – there was a new impetus in the arts. Not only were there some remarkable people in Leeds College of Art, but there was renewed vigour in the City Art Gallery with the appointment of Robert Rowe in 1958. At the University of Leeds, as well as an increasingly large number of talented and interesting people working there, the University now had the Gregory Fellows. Eric Gregory had founded and financed the Gregory Fellowships in 1949, which were administered by the University. A poet, sculptor and painter were invited to the University, where they could develop, and share their craft, be part of their Faculty, and yet independent of it.

Norbert Lynton, teaching history of art at Vernon Street, recalled that the Gregory Fellows 'felt rather isolated up the hill and soon came down it to the College of Art, finding that a much livelier centre. . . And Harry, of course, drew them in, involved them'.[17] The 'of course' is significant. This was Harry's way. Norbert himself had been drawn in, and was as involved in the new teaching as his colleagues in the studios and workshops. With this insight into Basic Research, he wrote to David Lewis:

The art student of today has to develop his own discipline: he has to discover his own direction out of self-knowledge, and during the whole of his career he will have to accept and reject what he chooses from the world around him. Do not expect him to be critical and selective in his art and at the same time to swallow unhesitatingly whatever in the way of culture and education you fling at him.[18]

What was flung at students at Vernon Street was unusual, certainly in the 1950s. In retrospect it may have seemed chaotic – one exciting event after another, experiment followed by innovation:

Not only nude models were used. Sometimes the model would be clothed, or half clothed. Sometimes some Indian dancers would appear with a couple of musicians playing an accompanying raga. Interjected between the colour exercises there might be a session, provided from the university or technical college, on the chemistry of pigments, or on the scientific basis of perception in optics. After a few days of hectic 9-5 work in the studio there might be a lecture or a group of lectures by someone from the University. Jerome Ravetz, a lecturer in the philosophy of science, gave a series of talks on the mathematical basis of forms in space, Asa Briggs on the history of Leeds, Richard Hoggart on popular culture, Ernst Gombrich or Basil Taylor might come up from London, Gombrich to talk on some aspect of the Renaissance or on the connections between art and information theory, Taylor to provide criticism of work being shown in the private London galleries.[19]

It is thought that Kenneth Armitage may have been the first of the Gregory Fellows to come 'down the hill', as a visiting artist from the University of Leeds to Vernon Street. In the following years Terry Frost, Alan Davie and Hubert (Nibs) Dalwood could each of them be found teaching at least one day a week at Leeds College of Art. Students were thought to benefit greatly through contact with practising artists. Terry Frost remembered: 'It was a fantastic period. Of course none of the students have ever forgotten that time. . . The whole thing was a studio with different attitudes and the same philosophical idea about it.'[20] And significantly, 'We were all finding out how to get the best out of each other.' He described how Harry Thubron would run a studio session and said, 'Anyway the thing was it was one of the best courses I've ever been involved in, I think we got it right.'[21]

The Director of Leeds City Art Gallery, Robert Rowe, wrote of 'that well-known and forward-looking College of Art', noting Taylor's calm leadership through unusual times.[22] Rowe arranged for Eric Taylor, and Quentin Bell at the University of Leeds, to be co-opted to the Gallery, Libraries and Arts Sub-Committee. Rowe wrote: 'Quentin Bell was to see that Taylor and I should be appointed to his University Advisory Committee and that Eric Taylor should master-mind the election of Quentin Bell and me as governors of the College of Art'. Rowe's three-way alliance (which he dubbed the Triumvirate), facilitated co-operation between the establishments. They also met and worked with Herbert Read,[23] described by his obituarist in 1968 as, 'the interpreter in England of specifically modern art'.[24] He was a national figure with a keen interest in the experiments taking place in Leeds.

Eric Taylor's son, Jan, who studied at the College, recalled that 'Herbert Read took an active interest [in the College] and was happy to lend his support to what was going on. Herbert Read was of some value in boosting morale at the College, some Schools Inspectors could be difficult'.[25] Michael, the son of Edward Pullée, quoted his father as saying, 'there were two very important influences in supporting Harry Thubron in his ideas and work, one was John Wood, and the other was Herbert Read.'[26]

Read was involved, too, with the selection of the Gregory Fellows, and he could see value in contact between them and Leeds College of Art. His publications *Education through Art* and *Art and Industry*,[27] at various times had

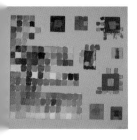

ABOVE AND RIGHT: TWO COLOUR EXERCISES BY CLIFF WOOD COMPLETED AS A STUDENT IN 1961
OIL ON CARD © THE ARTIST

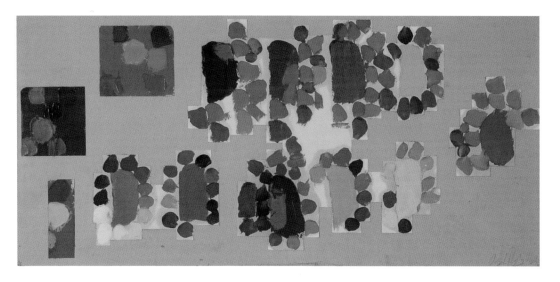

exercised considerable debate about the teaching of fine art. He was a committee member of the Leeds Arts Collection Fund, a group which made possible a number of important acquisitions for the collection of the City Art Gallery. Through these means he was able to provide a link between Leeds industrialists, their interest in contemporary painting and sculpture, and the art being produced in their own city. Read's presence also provided a connection to London and especially the Institute of Contemporary Art established in 1948.

By the early 1960s Thubron's position in Vernon Street and the Basic Design course itself seemed well established – interest and emulation could be found all round the country including London. When Thubron received an invitation from Edward Pullée to leave Leeds and to go to Lancaster College of Art, he was ready for the challenge. At Lancaster he was again to establish the Basic Research approach to teaching with some success as Jon Thompson, a teacher at Lancaster College of Art, observed, 'the sheer range and vitality of the work produced was without parallel in this country or abroad.'[28]

It is of dubious value to attempt to trace the origins of Harry Thubron's particular methods of teaching; its evolution and practice is too mercurial to pin to any sort of system. Norbert Lynton described Thubron's course as 'organic'. 'I watched Leeds students tackle the basic course over six years, each year it changed, each year it lost more of the original Bauhaus rigidity.'[29] Thubron delighted in Paul Klee's poetic dimension, studied Kandinsky, and was equally attracted to Sérusier on colour. 'I owe a great deal to de Sausmarez, (he translated Sérusier colour theory for me and the Bauhaus Kandinsky).'[30] Thubron saw in these artists qualities to inspire his own creativity and felt that others, including Victor Pasmore who adopted the Basic Design approach to his teaching, were too prescriptive. Thubron felt that Pasmore's differing interpretation of Klee's ideas, concentrating on the use of 'point and line to plane' was too much an instruction on 'how to do it'. Students remember Thubron's enthusiasm for Schwitters, Mondrian and Twombley, and his wide knowledge of contemporary art. Where he could, Thubron used the work of contemporary artists to illustrate an argument.

In spite of the elusive nature of human recollection, and Thubron's dislike of pedantry, much has been written about what happened during Thubron's nine years at the College of Art. What Thubron first called 'The Leeds Experiment' became Basic Research, a title used for a book accompanying an exhibition of students' work in 1962. Two years later the more familiar term Basic Design came into general usage following the publication of the Maurice de Sausmarez book bearing the phrase in its title. He wrote, 'I gratefully acknowledge all that I have gained from a long friendship with Harry Thubron whose work in Leeds and with Art Foundation, London, has contributed much to art education.'[31] In the Preface de Sausmarez stated, 'Emphatically this is not a primer in a special sort of art.'[32] But equally emphatically that is what it became to many readers. It satisfied their need for a system, and the belief that certain techniques could produce the desired work of art.

Anton Ehrenzweig, an educational psychologist who taught at Goldsmith's College, London, had for several years noticed the Intermediate students coming from Leeds College of Art for the unrepressed nature of their drawing. He called Harry Thubron 'the most inventive teacher in Britain.'[33] Ehrenzweig was impressed by Thubron's unique way of teaching, and became a close friend and ally. He saw that Basic Design changed as it became widely adopted, and he railed against its being used in a formulaic way.

To accompany an exhibition in 1981, at the Institute of Contemporary Arts in London, David Thistlewood wrote

A Continuing Process.[34] It had been intended to chart the progress and influence of the new approach to art teaching over twenty years. He speaks of the new creativity as occurring mainly in Newcastle and London, inspired by the teaching of Victor Pasmore, Richard Hamilton and Tom Hudson. Harry Thubron withdrew from this exhibition as he wrote to Victor Pasmore, 'we have a rough history according to Tom etc. Rubbish! . . . The difference between you and I was that I designed teams'. These remarks clearly show the different methodologies applied to basic research by these four exponents. In his introduction Thistlewood proposed that, 'If the present study makes only limited reference to Thubron, however, this is not because he is thought to have been less important (in fact he was inspirational and his efforts were formative) but because his philosophy merits quite separate consideration in a complementary exhibition.'

When Thubron left Leeds in 1964, Eric Atkinson was appointed Head of Painting at Vernon Street; he was himself to leave five years later to teach at Fanshawe College in Ontario, Canada. He took with him the methodology of Basic Research and his recollections of its special qualities are recorded in David Lewis' book *The Incomplete Circle*[35] published in 2000. The book contains a number of letters written to Lewis by colleagues of both Atkinson and Thubron from Vernon Street, which rekindle memories of the uniqueness of Basic Research.

Thubron's departure from Leeds was not allowed to disrupt the teaching practices at the College of Art. The teams at Leeds continued to work well, with Eric Atkinson as the new Head of Painting, in Vernon Street. In the late 1960s considerable confusion emerged about art education throughout the country, and in changes of structure and content in art courses. Government decisions about examinations and awards generated disappointment and disillusion among teachers. Yet in 1968, the *Yorkshire Evening Post* announced, 'Record Number of Honours at Leeds College of Art', noting that of the eighty diplomas awarded, twenty had achieved first-class honours. The diploma awards ceremony at Leeds City Art Gallery was presided over by Henri Henrion, the London-based design consultant for the 1951 Festival of Britain. He provided the following accolade, 'As far as I can see the work here is very much better than anywhere else in the country.'[36]

The impact of the encounters between tradition and innovation, which characterised, the Basic Design course, was felt beyond Vernon Street, and attracted national and international interest. 'The Leeds Experiment' led by Thubron and a dedicated group of teaching staff, provided a new way to approach creativity:

Maybe the real significance of what happened at Leeds lay in a recognition of the primacy of creative thinking in itself. . . staff and students alike were affected by an atmosphere of excitement, energy and imagination. An extra dimension was added by thoughts that all this was leading somewhere meaningful, that it was more than freedom for its own sake. That this sense of direction became increasingly fragmented is probably in the nature of things, and should not obscure the positive aspects of this legacy which still remain, nor detract from the tangible results of its influence, evident in so many creative endeavours throughout the country.[37]

In spite of the challenges it posed to the accepted practices in art education of the times, Basic Research succeeded within the very structures that tried to constrain it. It was a revolution that came from the studio floor, all-encompassing to those caught up in it, with reverberations far beyond Leeds.

The women's crafts, as they were described, weaving and embroidery, were with Miss Pugh and Miss Auty. There were three or four looms up in the attic, which also doubled as a common room. A not very strong Student Union had decided a common room was a necessity. It was very cramped in amongst the looms but we loved it. We had an old gramophone, a kettle and a gas ring!

We referred to the Teacher Training year as 'Pedagogy'. We did a whole day teaching in a school for the whole year. I did my practice at Cockburn High School, in Hunslet. . . No original ideas were needed from me. The Art Master always issued exact instructions as to 'what had to be done and how and with what. . .' On another afternoon of the week we went in a group to an elementary school. There we took it in turns at presenting and conducting a lesson. The rest of the group and our tutor (Mr Dixon) sat in the back row. Afterwards we had discussions on what had been done etc. It was very useful but quite frightening to perform in front of so many people. The rest of the week was spent in learning as many aspects of art and craft that were available in the College. We were warned that art teachers could be called upon to teach almost anything. So, we busied ourselves with bookbinding, 'women's crafts', sculpture, etching and jewellery. . . It was lovely, in the midst of war-time austerity, to be able to create rings, bracelets and brooches for oneself. . . Once a week we had a visit from a very magnificent lady who was a speech therapist. . . I forget her real name; we called her Madame O'Carty, after the character in Blithe Spirit, recently released as a film.

The new Principal was Edward E Pullée. He was a breath of fresh air. Magnificently moustached and often wearing a pink shirt, he resembled to me a circus ringmaster. He took great interest in the Teachers' Training course and talked about current educational trends and theories.

Another name of importance during that year was that of the HMI (His Majesty's Inspector) Mr Dalby. . . He was noted for his wit, which was very sharp and sarcastic and not to everyone's taste. I thought he was really entertaining. At the end of the year we were required to mount an exhibition of representative work; it had to include our own work and that of our pupils. We also had to write what we grandly called a thesis. The grand finale, as it were, was an interview with Mr Dalby.

MARGARET CORBIN (NÉE WALKER)
SEPTEMBER 1994
LEEDS COLLEGE OF ART STUDENT 1941-46

LEFT: LIFE PAINTING
BY PAT BURRAS, 1938
OIL ON CANVAS 91.2 x 70.5 CM
PRIVATE COLLECTION

After a period of evacuation from Leeds, I attained the Intermediate Art Scholarship in 1940. I believe that most students of eighteen years and over had left to join the Forces, leaving a relatively small number of younger students. Females considerably outnumbered males in my year. Our attitude to life was influenced by the troubled times and male students knew that call-up was inevitable.

We became immersed in drawing from plants, still-life and the Antique. In two rooms on the top floor was an arrangement of life-size plaster casts of Greek and Roman sculpture. I remember the Boy and Goose, the Belvedere Torso and Venus de Milo. The scale of these casts presented a challenge in assessing proportion. Here was where a learning process began and I did not find it easy to make a good drawing. The same problem awaited us in the large room next door where we drew from the male model, Mr O'Brian. He was a good model who held his pose well and I found the work more enjoyable. Our timetable also included theory and practice of colour, mechanical and free-hand perspective, and clay modelling.

The anatomy room on the first floor was complete with a human skeleton, plaster casts showing muscle structure, and wall charts. In the centre was a life model's throne. It was here that I drew my first female nude. I was somewhat embarrassed by the amused expressions on the faces of the female students as we three males entered the room.

Our teacher in life drawing was Percy Talbot ARCA. He taught us to look at the structure of the human figure and to represent it in a firm, simple, style. His manner was encouraging and his clear twinkling eyes hinted at a sense of humour. Quite his opposite in many ways was Mr TW Swindlehirst, a slim upright figure who, in his smart tailored suits, cut an elegant figure. A splash of colour from the ample ear of a silk handkerchief in his breast pocket completed the effect. 'Tommy', as we referred to him privately, taught me the refinements of the letterform.

John Greenwood RE RBA ARCA and Head of Design, was a somewhat enigmatic, and puckish person. . . He could be very complimentary. 'I wish I had done that,' he once said to me, which both startled and pleased me. And, to a piece I had done with which he disapproved, his remark, 'So what!', proved quite thought provoking – and salutary.

Mr Houghton taught me illustration. With hair tending to fall over his cheeks, a beard, and plus-fours, he was the only member of staff resembling an artist. . . Architecture was taught by Mr Waite supported by our bible of tome proportions written by Sir Banister Fletcher. . . Modelling in clay was the province of Mr Bissett, a talented Scottish sculptor. A small man wearing a sculptor's smock, he demonstrated the principle of three-dimensional form by drawing profiles of the human figure on the blackboard. The outline of the complete figure was drawn in one continuous line with a balletic movement of his arm.

As it was wartime some of our time was spent colouring the land features of Ordnance Survey maps connected with the war effort. A rota was drawn up of students who were willing to do fire-watching. . . Stirrup pumps, buckets for water and buckets for sand stood at the ready to extinguish small fires and incendiary bombs.

Following demobilisation I continued my studies and was helped by a small ex-serviceman's grant. . . The College interior retained its rather drab institutional colouring. . . Starting again was an unsettling experience.

The year I studied in the Teacher Training Department (1952-3) was the most demanding in my career as a student. There was almost a competitive element in the standards for which we were striving because vacancies in art teaching were sparse.

The Head of the Department was Cyril Cross who presided over a small team of lecturers as a priest over disciples. Cyril proved to be an inspiring leader who taught us to think of the needs of our pupils as a central theme behind our teaching. I was often enthralled by the shining examples of art, which emerged through our teaching projects and appreciated that these qualities would be reflected in classrooms of the future.

ALWYN JOSEPH DOYLE
NOVEMBER 1994
LEEDS COLLEGE OF ART STUDENT 1940-42, 1946-48 AND 1952-53

LEFT: LIFE STUDY
BY STUART CAMPBELL, C1937
INK 39.2 x 17.8 CM
PRIVATE COLLECTION

Firm Foundations
The Process Continues

Chris Owen

FIRM FOUNDATIONS
THE PROCESS CONTINUES

CHRIS OWEN

Enter Vernon Street today, and the scene which meets your eyes seems far removed from the days of Harry Thubron and the Basic Design movement.[1] Students now fill every nook and cranny of the old building, and they can rarely afford the time to conduct visual research in the ways that Thubron encouraged in the 1950s. But these differences mask a story of remarkable continuity within the building. Vernon Street annually houses over 200 students studying the Art and Design Foundation course, which was established nationally in 1961 and is based on the principles of the Basic Design movement. The Foundation course has over this period become an important staging post in the careers of young British artists and designers. It has survived all kinds of threats to its existence – ideological, financial, and educational.

The distinctive pedagogy of the Foundation course has never been easily absorbed into the structures of the educational system. Yet the Foundation course has survived, in something resembling its original state, as a diagnostic course preparing post-A level students for undergraduate level studies in art and design. The intention of this study is to analyse the historical development of the Foundation course, and the course as it exists today, in order to determine whether it is essentially the same course as that devised in the 1950s, or whether it has evolved into a fundamentally different experience. In short, is the Foundation course at Vernon Street today a modernist relic, which deserves to be buried with dignity? Or does it still provide a vibrant and relevant experience to contemporary students – the artists and designers of the twenty-first century?

When the National Advisory Council on Art Education revised the structure of British art education in 1960 (the First Coldstream Report), it was part of a concerted effort to raise the standards of design education. The previous system – a two-year Intermediate Certificate followed by a two-year National Diploma in Design (NDD) – was considered insufficient to produce professional artists and designers. Many students with GCE A levels

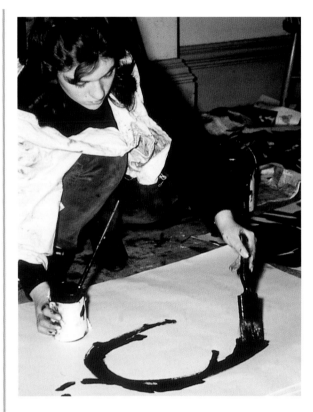

progressed directly to the NDD, and those with the Certificate lacked the rigorous academic training of A levels. The new DipAD, replacing the NDD, was to last three years, and entrants were expected to be not less than eighteen and to 'have produced evidence of ability in art and have reached a satisfactory standard in general education.'[2]

Coldstream also determined that a new Pre-Diploma course, of one year, would in most cases be completed between school and the DipAD course – the beginning of the Art and Design Foundation course. In 1961 Basic Design courses, which had been pioneered at Leeds by Harry Thubron and at Newcastle by Victor Pasmore and Richard Hamilton, would cease to be the pioneering experiments of individual art educators in the provinces. For the first time, they were to become institutionalized within the structures of government policy on art education, and controlled from London.

The content of the Pre-Diploma course was described in fairly general terms, but was clearly based on Basic Design principles:

The general aim of all these courses should be to train students in observation, analysis, creative work and technical control through the study of line, form, colour and space relationships in two and three dimensions. A sound training in drawing is implicit in all these studies. All courses should include some study of the history of art and some complementary studies.[3]

In the early sixties, these aims were not well understood, or were resisted, in some colleges. But at Leeds, the principles had already been well established by Harry Thubron before the new course was instituted. A summary of topics covered by the basic course was presented in the College prospectus as early as 1958.

2D Exercises

1 Lines
2 Planes
3 Free Spatial Relationships of a Given Rectilinear Area
4 Development of Primary Forms and Other Complementaries
5 Colour Analysis
6 Analytical Drawing from Natural Forms

3D Exercises

7 Colour Analysis in Spatial Relationships
8 Development of Cubic Relationship in Mass
9 Spatial Division and Light Relationships with Rectilinear Planes
10 Spatial Division in Relationship with Straight Lines
11 Spatial Relationship in Curvilinear Forms leading to Spherical Construction [4]

In the same prospectus, Thubron explained how the new approach would give a foundation in the visual elements to all art and design students, in a statement reminiscent of Walter Gropius' original vision for the pre-war Bauhaus:

It has been decided in the Leeds schools that from their very first term onwards, students of painting, architecture, sculpture and industrial design shall be taught together as far as possible and practicable; sharing the same workrooms, and the same visual problems.

In this way they will grow aware of the common ground which all share, rather than of their differences; and from this awareness the much needed integration of visual professions in contemporary life, at the present so lacking, will be encouraged through the encouragement at student level of mutual understanding, sympathy and co-relation.

Concerning this question of 'integration'. . . we wish to stimulate co-operation in the most active and enlightened sense between builders, designers, and creative artists.[5]

Just three years later, something very similar to this Basic Design course was accepted nationally as a valuable preparation for art and design higher education.

The Pre-Diploma changed its name to the Foundation course following an addendum to the Coldstream Report, published in 1965 in response to the First Report of the National Council for Diplomas in Art and Design (NCDAD – the Summerson Council) in 1964. The addendum reiterated word for word the guidelines on curriculum of five years before, as quoted above. But the addendum also made clear the liberal philosophy and fear of a new academicism based on abstraction, which were characteristic of art educators of the time:

Although we recognize that a measure of uniformity might be achieved by a form of central approval of pre-diploma studies, we have no doubt that the best interests of art education would not be served by this form of control. We therefore remain strongly of the opinion that art schools should be free to construct and direct their own courses.[6]

Ironically, the addendum coincided with the publication of several new books on Basic Design, which threatened to impose precisely this kind of standardised curriculum. In particular, *Basic Design: the Dynamics of Visual Form*, published in 1964 by Maurice de Sausmarez, a close associate of Thubron, became a virtual textbook for Foundation courses throughout the country. As will be argued later, it is by avoiding this tendency to codify a set syllabus, in order to retain the underlying principles of the pedagogy, that teachers of the Foundation course have been able to retain the relevance and vibrancy of the programme over forty years.

By the mid-sixties, many of the originators of the Basic Design movement and their followers – including Thubron – had moved to other colleges, helping to spread the

Basic Design message. There was soon little to distinguish the course at Leeds from that at Leicester College of Art and Design, or London's Royal College of Art.[7] A detailed syllabus plan, now in the National Art Education Archive at Bretton Hall, was written by Tom Hudson, a colleague of Thubron, probably after he had left Leeds and was working at Leicester. Most noticeable is the length of the exercises; two weeks spent exploring the development of planes in three dimensions, two more on form and mass. Five different types of drawing are distinguished, and prescribed 'throughout the year'. General education was delivered by visiting lecturers, covering subjects as diverse as astronomy, biology, ethics and poetry.[8]

One significant feature of the Foundation course, which was first clearly defined in the 1965 Addendum, was its diagnostic function. The early courses of Pasmore, Hamilton and Thubron were envisaged as a broad education in visual studies, but the process by which specialisation would be achieved was vague. Pasmore viewed the Foundation course as essential for fine artists, Hamilton for all designers.[9] Pasmore also believed that the course was not just an introduction, but part of the continuing process of developing as an artist. As he put it thirty years later: 'In no sense of the word is it a first year course. I'm still doing it.' [10]

The idea that through Basic Design a student would learn which art or design discipline they were best suited to, and gradually concentrate their efforts in this area, had not previously been made explicit. Nor, apparently, did it happen at first. Derek Page, the current Foundation Course Leader at Vernon Street, was himself an early student on the course at Leeds. He contrasts the original aims with the diagnostic focus of the course today:

There was absolutely no indication of even the kind of rudimentary way you'd tackle diagnostic courses. . . It was assumed that you would find the path, in some mysterious way, and people did go on to do graphics, went on to do this, that and the other. But, from my recollection, there was nothing about a member of staff sitting down with you and going through the work and looking for the kind of clues that we look for now.[11]

The NACAE Addendum made the diagnostic function a central role of the Foundation course:

There is a brief reference in our First Report to the diagnostic function of pre-diploma courses which needs to be emphasized. These courses should help teachers and students to discover the latter's potentialities and the direction in which they can best be developed.[12]

This change of emphasis forced each college to remove any lingering vestiges of their old 'two-plus-two' year programme, and create a clearly delineated, but integrated, structure of Foundation plus three years. The increase nationally in higher education maintenance grants, and in the range of new art and design DipAD courses, meant the diagnostic function of the Foundation course had to become its most significant feature. For the first time, students could use this year to make genuine choices about what they wished to specialize in, and where. The DipAD courses were divided into four main curriculum areas – fine art, graphics, 3D and fashion/textiles. On Foundation, the NACAE stated: 'Opportunity should be taken during the course to make students aware of the full range of studies available in diploma courses in all four areas.' [13]

The change of name, from Pre-Diploma to Foundation, was also intended to ensure that students did not see progression to the College's own DipAD as an automatic process. Foundation was to act as a diagnostic filter through to a national network of specialist art and design courses, which themselves were soon to attain degree status.

This directive changed the Foundation course from a full year of Basic Design and drawing to a structure in which Basic Design exercises were reduced to fill only the first few weeks, and diagnostic exercises completed the first half of the year. Students then specialized in one discipline area, and built a portfolio for Higher Education application. This revised syllabus and methodology became standard in many colleges by the early seventies. The curriculum is still much the same today. This development dramatically shifted the aim of the Foundation course away from the concept which the Basic Design pioneers had developed from the Bauhaus – the art school as a laboratory for pure visual experimentation. From this point on, the purpose of the Foundation course was the early diagnosis of design skills, and the development of vocational specialisation.

By the mid-seventies, the Foundation course was well established around the country. The new polytechnic sector, controlled by the CNAA, had been established to offer degree courses in vocational subjects. Art and design colleges had been either incorporated into these new institutions (as at Leicester), or divided into an independent FE art college and an HE department within a polytechnic (Leeds). The division at Leeds in 1970 moved the DipAD courses to the new polytechnic, but left the Foundation course at Vernon Street. The change upset all staff – those who moved to the polytechnic felt they had lost their art school, and those who remained in the college of art mourned the loss of the higher level courses. The split is remembered by some with bitterness even today.

At the end of 1970, the National Council for Diplomas in Art and Design (the Summerson Committee), and the National Advisory Council on Art Education, chaired by Sir William Coldstream, issued a joint report, which attempted in considerable detail to clarify the whole art and design post-sixteen education system. On Foundation courses, this Second Coldstream Report identified four key areas of concern, which can be summarised thus:

1 The growth of Foundation courses had outpaced DipAD, leading to nearly two Foundation students chasing each Diploma place

2 Some Foundation courses were fine art orientated, and ignored their diagnostic function

3 Because applications were being made before Easter, the Foundation course did not give sufficient time to diagnose potential as well as providing a broad visual education

4 Standards and course content were too diverse, and central guidance was needed to maintain consistency [14]

The report noted that general education entry standards had improved between 1963 and 1969 (in 1962 26% of students had two A levels compared to 44% in 1969), and that most students were now completing two years of sixth form study before specializing in art and design at the age of nineteen. The report therefore recommended that the majority of students should continue to complete A levels, Foundation and then a three-year HE course. The report also paved the way for splitting existing DipAD courses into two categories. Group A were to remain three-year courses, and would normally be preceded by Foundation. These courses would quickly convert to BA status. Group B courses, of four-year duration, would more likely be entered directly from school at sixteen, and would be more vocational.

This Second Coldstream Report provoked a mixed response. Many art educators felt the report's promotion of the existing Foundation system would strengthen their position, but others saw dangers in the way Foundation was becoming primarily diagnostic, and in the separation of academic and vocational diplomas. Eric Taylor, a very able administrator, had moved from his post as Principal at Leeds College of Art to be Assistant Director of Leeds Polytechnic in 1970. He resigned from the Summerson Committee and took early retirement, in protest at the way he saw the basic principles of art education being undermined by the emphasis on vocation and career structures. In his view, the Bauhaus principle of integrating art and design was under threat, as he claimed in his resignation speech. To reinforce this message, he quoted the Second Coldstream Report's assertion that 'we would not now regard the study of fine art as necessarily central to all studies in the design field.' [15]

By early 1973, the NCDAD were planning for the DipAD courses to be granted BA (Hons) status, and for their own amalgamation as the Board of Studies for Art and Design, within the CNAA. For these things to happen, the requirement for students to have appropriate academic qualifications had to be insisted upon. The Council issued a memorandum on the future preparation and entry of students. From now on, progression to DipAD courses would require 'a General Certificate of Education with passes in five subjects, including two subjects at advanced level'.[16]

The memorandum pointed out that provision other than A levels for students of art and design aged sixteen to eighteen was not yet of sufficient depth or quality to legitimize progression to BA (Hons) standard courses. The Council saw little option, therefore, but to insist on A levels as a pre-requisite for the DipAD courses, if they were to be allowed to change to BA (Hons) status. The memorandum recognized, however, the concerns of many lecturers, that academic A levels were not necessarily always the best training for their particular higher education disciplines:

It is a natural assumption that in the great majority of cases at least one of the A levels or equivalent qualifications will be in the art/design area, and for those whose interests in this field are all consuming there is no reason why both should not be.[17]

This new regulation created considerable anguish within art and design educational institutions. This was exacerbated when local education authorities added to the call for standardisation across HE by recommending that the high staff/student ratios of art colleges be brought down to the same level as those in engineering and technology. Much of the anger was fuelled by fear of changes which were not formally being proposed. It was assumed that because so much of the agenda was concerned with standardising sixth form and higher education across disciplines, the anomalous position of the Foundation course, between two years of A levels and a three-year degree, would inevitably jeopardise its survival. These fears eventually proved unfounded. Nevertheless, the fact that other subject areas are not provided with a one-year bridging course between A levels and degree courses has been raised by critics at regular intervals ever since.

Foundation courses eventually succumbed to calls for a regulatory system in the early 1980s, by creating a form of self-regulation, in which regional consortia of colleges (at Leeds – YHAFHE) provided cross-moderation. In the process, staff from different colleges developed a greater understanding of each other, and formed a powerful

ABOVE: SPATIAL EXERCISE, DRAW WALL AND FLOOR, FOUNDATION C EARLY PROJECTS, 1994 © LEEDS COLLEGE OF ART AND DI

lobbying group. Only in the early 1990s did Foundation courses yield to the demands for external national recognition, under the aegis either of their own awarding body, the National Board for Foundation Studies in Art and Design (NBFSAD), or of BTEC (now Edexcel). These bodies ensured that Foundation courses responded to changes elsewhere in FE, and encouraged greater standardisation, through syllabus guidelines and adherence to nationally agreed assessment procedures.

Throughout this period, supporters of the Foundation philosophy have resisted pressures to compromise their principles. The requirements to diagnose potential and develop a portfolio within two terms have not dissipated. The self-criticism necessitated by the self-regulation processes in many ways strengthened the arguments for the Foundation course, and refined the methodology of Foundation teachers. The economic pressures on Foundation courses have ensured that they become ever more professional and efficient. Gone are the days of eight-to-one student/staff ratios and thirty hours teaching per week for students. The initiation of students into new ways of approaching visual form and design problems now has to be achieved in large groups within a very short space of time. Rigorous analysis of how the process works has enabled Foundation tutors to hone the curriculum into something more reminiscent of an efficient production line than a profound educational experience. Resistance to change in basic principles has never been stronger. But it is a deep understanding of these principles, and refusal to compromise on them, that has allowed teaching staff to adapt to ever tighter economic conditions, without standards appearing to diminish appreciably.

Many of the critical changes to Foundation over the last twenty years have arisen not from within the courses themselves, but through external influences from the political, educational and cultural context in which they operate. In particular, the Foundation course has lost its position as the sole access route into UK art and design undergraduate education.

The inability of the art education community to develop a credible lower level alternative to Foundation had left a gap in provision which needed to be filled. Two-year versions of Foundation, to cater for the 'exceptional'

non-A level student, and for the sixteen-year-old school leaver, had never been well-structured or methodically regulated. Often these students were offered little more than the chance to do the Foundation year twice, with A level Art thrown in as a bonus at the end of the first year. One answer to this problem was the four-year sub-degree vocational courses, established in 1970 and mostly taken by school leavers at sixteen. These courses were incorporated in the early 1980s into the new Business and Technician Education Council (BTEC). They became National Diploma and Higher National Diploma courses. For the first time, the structure and assessment practices of art college FE courses were determined not solely by art educators, but by the imposition of a national framework, and its methodology was derived from industrial training models.

The BTEC pattern of two-year National Diploma plus two-year HND became, by the late eighties, a familiar and popular alternative to Foundation plus degree, particularly for students lacking the academic skills to cope with A levels. For the most part, these were specialist vocational courses, for example in graphic design or fashion, lacking a diagnostic art and design function. Inherent in their philosophy was the idea that students had a choice after ND – higher education, or a technician job in the design industry. Higher education invariably meant HND in the

1980s for these students. Amongst these specialist courses, however, a General Art and Design ND was also introduced (GAD). Although the diagnostic process was similar, GAD was based on a different philosophy to Foundation. Drawing and visual studies were conceived as modules of a two-year programme which taught a range of art and design skills, in order to develop students' understanding of their vocational direction. The conceptual and philosophical framework of the Foundation course was for the most part missing. The unitised structure allowed students to develop segments of knowledge and expertise for specific ends, whereas Foundation still viewed the creative process as holistic and experimental.

In the early 1990s, GAD was transformed into GNVQ Advanced Art and Design. The philosophy was again derived from industrial training methods, and for the first time a standardised syllabus was dictated centrally; individual centres could no longer design their own courses. The assessment process, based on demonstrating competence in design skills, was alien to the principles of many art educators, and served to demonstrate clearly the philosophical difference between Foundation and this new diagnostic alternative. In 2000, the GNVQ Advanced was converted into the AVCE or Vocational A level course, but the methodology was not changed significantly. In Leeds, the Vernon Street building still mainly houses the Foundation course at Leeds College of Art and Design. But it is now linked by a courtyard and bridge to its sister building in Rossington Street, where an almost equal number of AVCE students are taught.

Another route into HE has developed for adults – the Access course. Its philosophy is rooted in community education, and again it demonstrates an alternative assessment methodology to Foundation. By the end of the 1990s, adults returning to education had grown into a significant educational market. In Leeds, there was no longer room to house all these students at Vernon Street. Since the mid-1980s, Leeds College of Art and Design's second site, at Blenheim Walk, has grown to accommodate many students from these alternative courses. There are now over 150 adult students on Access courses each year at the Blenheim Walk site.

This diversification of art and design further education provided considerable competition to the Foundation

course for students. It also helped to demystify the Foundation course philosophy, by demonstrating to art and design staff how the personal and profound experience of art education could be rationalized into precise learning objectives and assessed according to clear criteria.

Throughout the 1990s, the Government agenda of expanding higher education provided ever greater opportunities for the students on the new feeder courses to enter higher education. The intense competition for places which had prevented most ND students from progressing to degree courses in the 1980s diminished rapidly. It became increasingly common for students from AVCE and ND courses to compete with Foundation students for places on the best BA (Hons) courses. Leeds College of Art and Design developed a range of new undergraduate courses throughout the mid/late 1990s, to fill the gap left when the original college was split in 1970. By 2003, the College was catering for over 600 HE students on a wide range of specialist courses. Meanwhile the courses established at Leeds Polytechnic, which is now Leeds Metropolitan University, also continue to flourish. After all this growth, a typical design degree first year starting in 2003 will contain a mix of students from A level, Foundation, AVCE, National Diploma and Access routes. The students from these varying backgrounds have equivalent qualifications, but they have been taught to approach art and design in quite different ways.

As pressures for efficiency have grown, and deregulation has affected both FE and HE, students from the best Foundation courses have become even more popular with undergraduate teaching staff. Competitive pressures have encouraged Foundation staff to push students to specialize earlier. BA course leaders also respond favourably to students who seem to have already learned how to think creatively. This process is self-perpetuating. The BA courses favour students with more specialized portfolios, and the Foundation courses specialize earlier to produce them. It might also be argued that as higher education becomes an ever more expensive undertaking, the Foundation course caters primarily for privileged students, who have completed A levels, and can afford to take an extra year to prepare themselves for HE. The Foundation course at Leeds has established a high reputation for success in this process, and now

increasingly attracts many of its students from a national and international market.

As Eric Taylor had predicted, the process of vocational specialisation has put ever greater strain on the basic design/visual exploration content, which formed the core of the original Foundation course. At Leeds, as at all other colleges, the Foundation course is now divided into three stages – Visual Language, Specialisation, and Final Project/Exhibition. The first stage lasts just eleven weeks. The course content has been simplified, so that what was originally a year of educational development in the elements of visual form can now be condensed into less than three months.

This reduction in the emphasis on visual studies might appear to signal a major shift in approach, away from the original Basic Design movement. At a fundamental level, however, the process is a continuing one. Thubron, Pasmore and Hamilton created an approach which opposed the outdated and academic art and design education of the immediate post-war period. Their pedagogy was based on nurturing creativity rather than teaching craft skills, and it reflected the principles and

processes common to all areas of contemporary practice. Exploration of visual form was the key common concern of the art and design practice of the 1950s. From abstract expressionism in painting to the international modernist style in architecture, an essential creative starting point was the exploration and understanding of the abstract elements of art and design. Even then, in Newcastle Richard Hamilton also insisted on the importance of technology and new philosophical ideas in the development of the artist or designer's ideas. And in Leeds, Thubron encouraged contributions from psychologists, sociologists and mathematicians to his new course. Since the 1950s, art and design practice has embraced a broader range of creative starting points, and so the Foundation course has followed suit. Contemporary art and design practices arise from the imagery and ideas of a global information culture, while contemporary design methodology is often based on problem-solving as much as visual experimentation. The Foundation course has adapted to these new realities, in order to maintain its contemporary relevance.

In 2001, Foundation courses across the country were revised, and ironically this educational structure which had always resisted regulation and uniformity became one of the first courses in the country to be standardised within the Government's new National Qualifications Framework. At a series of regional forums to discuss the proposals, it was stressed that the aim of the new course specifications was to 'retain the characteristics of thirty years development and practice – progressive, cumulative development of the student.'[18]

This review provides an opportunity to compare the new Foundation course syllabus with Harry Thubron's basic course from 1958. The exercise demonstrates clearly how sophisticated the analysis of the educational process has become over the last forty years. The BTEC Diploma in Foundation Studies (Art and Design) consists of nine units, in three stages. There is no requirement to teach the units separately. In place of the visual elements specified for exploration in the 1950s (Line, Colour Analysis, etc), each unit explores an aspect of the design process:

STAGE ONE – EXPLORATORY STAGE

Unit 1   Information and Research
Unit 2   Recording and Responding
Unit 3   Media Experimentation

STAGE TWO – PATHWAY STAGE

Unit 4   Information and Interpretation
Unit 5   Combined Experimental Studies
Unit 6   Media Development
Unit 7   Preparation and Progression

STAGE THREE – CONFIRMATORY STAGE

Unit 8   Integrating Theory and Practice
Unit 9   Personal Confirmatory Study [19]

The unit outlines do not prescribe curriculum content. For example, 'Information and Research' is explained in the full course document as introducing the student to 'attitudes and processes that will enable them to foster their own creativity and engage in self-reliant learning'. Under a section in this module on skills, knowledge and understanding, are listed 'visual and textual research techniques', and 'identifying how to develop creativity by taking risks'.

Learning outcomes and assessment criteria have been carefully conceived to retain the character of the original Foundation experience; one example is 'suspend judgement, in order to open out the field of enquiry into the unfamiliar'[20] – a distant echo of Victor Pasmore's exhortation to 'forget everything you. . . ever learned about art and start from the beginning.'[21] In this way, the process of creativity is being further deconstructed into its component skills, for the purposes of assessment. The content may not be specified, but the general aims of the original Basic Design movement are being maintained, and spelt out in detail. Above all, the specifications retain the aim of the originators of the Foundation course – 'a general devotion to the principle of individual creative development.'[22] The aims of the new Foundation course are couched as generalisations, in order to retain the experimental approach of the student experience, and to encourage individual innovation in the teaching process itself.

The new Foundation course attempts to retain the fundamental principles of the old Basic Design course, embrace the advances made in analysing the stages of the design process and their teaching, and to express all this in a language and within a structure dictated by the New Qualifications Framework. In so doing, it demonstrates clearly how the Foundation course has been continually developed and adapted by its practitioners over the last forty years. The Vernon Street building has proved to be remarkably well-designed, architecturally, to foster the education of artists and designers over a hundred years, however the demands of that education may change. The Foundation course which inhabits Vernon Street, has proved to be equally adaptable over the last forty years. It might even be fair to say that its educational principles are based on similarly firm foundations.

RIGHT: FOUNDATION COURSE FINAl
MAJOR PROJECT, FINE ART PATHWA
PHOTOGRAPHIC STUDY BASED ON
VERNON STREET STAIRWELL BY
KIRSTEN DOBLE 2002
© LEEDS COLLEGE OF ART AND DESI

My parents were middle-class in the sense that my father wore a white shirt to work every day – but working class in terms of income and aspirations. Therefore, as a grammar school pupil, I was ordered to study science, work hard, and was left in no doubt that after school came a proper job. Further education was not presented as an option.

The First Day: Here is a bunch of young people gathered together for the first time in Jacob Kramer; the Art Foundation students 1975/76. And me. Feeling very out of place.

Our lecturers make some general introductions, and then announce some 'ice-breaking' exercises. One of these is a kind of 'ring o' roses' game in which the students form a spiral chain, becoming gradually tighter.

And it so happens that I am right at the centre of this coil. A person who, a few weeks before, had been working on a building site in the company of macho Sun readers, who would be more likely to walk on the moon than tolerate a situation like this. As panic sets in I begin to think that somehow I have been transported back in time to my nursery school. I have to get out of that mass of bodies and jump onto a table. At the top of my voice I shout 'Stop!' The place goes very quiet and I step down from the table.

The man who had organised this childish exercise seemed very amused by my outburst and later I thought it might have appealed to his sense of anarchy. His name was Patrick Oliver, an imposing figure in a formidable team of lecturers. His appearance was distinctly (and I assume deliberately) grubby. Tall and skinny, his uncombed greasy hair, dirty fingers, a soiled waxed jacket and a furious smoking habit gave him the aura of a malevolent scarecrow.

Patrick's humour was sardonic and his attitude contrary. He would routinely challenge and debunk any given popularly-held belief. Although I was wary of him, I enjoyed his outrageous views, because they made me think. At the earliest opportunity he declared that we had to unlearn everything we had been taught about art, which was okay by me as I knew nothing.

Patrick's co-conspirator that day was Kate Russell, the only female member of staff on the course. A graphic designer by training, she had a knowledge of typography, which was a new subject to me. I remember particularly a great talk she gave on the elegant design of the London Underground map. She also encouraged us to obtain small notebooks and draw, write or doodle in them every day. This I did and found it to be a great and rewarding discipline.

The Experience: I adored the building. A big sprawling, magnificent old place which incorporated a theatre and a music college. Often I could hear the sound of students rehearsing jazz in a far-off room, while I was scribbling a life drawing in charcoal, the medium of choice on the course.

There were two main studios – old, high, paint-splattered and cold. I felt very at home in those big rooms. For me they generated a sense of chaos and innovation, which I was very comfortable with. That things might be created out of nothing was a powerful idea, which stayed with me. I loved to be there. Perhaps it was the smell. A mixture of oil paint, sawdust, glue and cheap hairspray.

One day a visiting lecturer turned up to teach a week-long class on video production. He brought with him a Sony Portapak, a revolutionary piece of equipment, which triggered the video art movement. The lecturer was Steve Bell, who later created the 'If. . .' cartoon strip. That week changed my life and video became a passion, which endured.

I shall be forever grateful to the College for revealing a world which I might have otherwise missed. So thanks to all those mentioned here and many others who made that year so magical.

JOHN ADAMS
SEPTEMBER 2003
LEEDS COLLEGE OF ART STUDENT 1975-76

LEFT: FOUNDATION COURSE FINAL
MAJOR PROJECT, TEXTILES PATHWAY;
STUDY FOR AN INSTALLATION BY
KATHERINE HYDE, 2002
© LEEDS COLLEGE OF ART AND DESIGN

The Process Continues
LEEDS COLLEGE OF ART AND DESIGN, FOUNDATION COURSE 2003

It's like complicated, serious and difficult play school because you have to look so deep into such simple things. Strange!
ANON.

Haven't started seeing the world completely in dots and lines, but feel I could if I wanted to.

I used to consider myself an artist, but I've found I can't even get marks on a page right.
JESS PAMPHLETT

Like being kidnapped by a cult. Teachers speak like the initiated. Occasionally ingenious, frequently silly, schoolish, linguistically challenged but brings out unexpected magic.
ROSE-ANNA BLEASDALE

eclectic	*theatrical*	*the fount of all my gladness*
weird	*edwardian*	*smokin!*
knackering	*mind-bending*	*delightful*
new!	*rhythmic*	*metric*
thrilling	*foundation-tastic*	
obligatory	*depressing*	
funky	*demoralising*	
	humiliating	

KEIRA MILLER, LAUREN FEAR, SUSANNAH RUMSBY

I've always loved integrity of work but never been taught that it's important whereas here everything is about integrity and crafting, showing the love and energy that people put into their art as essentially valuable. I value drawing (line) a lot more as well and the 3D hinging/expansion have both made me question my methods.
THOMAS WALKER

It's been crazy. Who'd have thought you could fit so much into one week. I've spent all my free time sleeping!
AGGIE BAINBRIDGE

It has made me realise that everything is not as it may first seem, something simple has potential as a complex form, simply by changing the way we view an object, a surface or a line can also affect the way it reads.
LEILA OMIDVAR

I feel my perspective on art and design has changed. The world feels like a mesh of abstraction.
KIMLEE MILLER

Felt as if I had been thrown in the deep end without armbands, but the world makes you forget that it is possible and beneficial to sometimes do that. . .
Makes you realise just how safety and security conscious the world is, instead of being prepared to take risks, not knowing where you are going.
ANON.

LEFT: DOUBLE ACTION DRAWING TOOLS
MADE AND USED BY FOUNDATION
COURSE STUDENTS, 2001
© LEEDS COLLEGE OF ART AND DESIGN

AUTHORS' NOTES

DAVID BOSWELL, ARTS WITH CRAFTS

1 Quentin Bell, *The Schools of Design* (London: Routledge and Kegan Paul, 1963)
Stuart Macdonald, *The History and Philosophy of Art Education* (London: University of London, 1970)
Christopher Frayling, *The Royal College of Art: one hundred and fifty years of Art and Design* (London: Barrie and Jenkins, 1987)
2 Owen Jones, *The Grammar of Ornament* (London: Day and Son, 1856)
3 Leeds Institute of Science, Art and Literature (LI), *Historical Sketch 1824-1900* (1901). Several later short histories of the School update this.
Rebecca Lowe, *Past into Present: a Commemorative History of Leeds College of Art and Design* (Leeds: Leeds College of Art and Design, 1993)
See Macdonald, *op. cit.* note 1, pp167, 217, 255-6
4 Leeds Institute School of Art Sub-Committee (LIS of AS): *Minutes* (19 November 1886)
5 LI: *Annual Report for 1889* (1890) p12
6 LI: *Annual Report for 1892* (1893) p10
7 *Yorkshire Evening Post* (2 June 1906)
8 LI: *Annual Report for 1893* (1894) p9
9 LI: *Annual Report for 1899* (1900) p10
10 LI: *Annual Report for 1900* (1901) p12
11 Frayling, *op. cit.* note 1, p66
John Swift, 'The Arts and Crafts Movement at Birmingham Art School 1880-1900' in David Thistlewood, (ed), *Histories of Art and Design: Cole to Coldstream* (London: Longmans, 1992) pp23-37
Stuart Macdonald, 'Newbery and "The Four": a School for Europe' in Thistlewood, *op. cit.* pp80-104
12 Basil H Jackson (ed), *Recollections of Thomas Graham Jackson 1835-1924* (London: Oxford University, 1950) p261
13 LI, *Proposed New School of Art: Instructions to Architects*, p3, with *Schedule of Requirements* (1901)
14 William H Bidlake, *Assessor's Report: the Leeds School of Art* (1901) pp1 and 4
Michael Jackson, 'William Henry Bidlake 1861-1938', *RIBA West Midlands Yearbook* (Birmingham, 1999) pp8-10
15 West Yorkshire Archive Service, *Building Plan Register 1901*, No. 61, p224. *New Art School 30 August 1901*, set of six plans from Bedford and Kitson dated 23 August 1901
LI, *Calendar and Syllabus: 1904-5* (1904) p113
16 Macdonald, *op. cit.* note 1, pp184-5
Ann Levitt, *An Analysis of the Development of Construction Project Management*, (Birmingham: University of Central England, unpublished Diploma thesis in CPM, 1992) Appendix 1. Case study/School of Art (by Martin and Chamberlain)
Thomas Haworth, *Charles Rennie Mackintosh and the Modern Movement* (London: Routledge and Kegan Paul, 1952) pp69-92
17 Hermann Muthesius, *The English House* (London: Crosby, Lockwood, Staples, 1979). English translation from German volumes of 1904-5
18 Leeds School of Art (LS of A) in connection with LI, *New Building Scheme* 'Current Architecture: Leeds School of Art', *Architectural Review 15* (1904) pp164-9
19 LI, 'Appendix: New School of Art Foundation Stone Ceremony', *Annual Report for 1901* (1902) pp23-27
20 Bedford and Kitson, *New School of Art: Estimate for Furniture, Screens and Panelling* (February 1903)
21 LI, *Address by Ernest W Beckett, Esq, M.M. on 'Art Culture' at the opening of the New School of Art* (8 October 1903)
22 LS of A, *Opening of the New Building* (8 October 1903)
23 LI, *Annual Report for 1902* (1903) pp13-14
24 LI, *Calendar for 1904-5* (1904) p104
25 LI, *Calendar for 1904-5* (1904) p118
26 Tom Steele, *Alfred Orage and the Leeds Arts Club 1893-1923* (Aldershot: Scolar Press, 1999) pp 4-5. From the Club's records, Steele thought it had arranged the exhibition but the correspondence in the City Art Gallery's files indicate that its sub-committee was the leading organiser
27 Elizabeth Knowles, *Dod Procter RA (1892-1972) Ernest Procter (1886-1935)* (Newcastle-upon-Tyne: Laing Gallery, 1990)
28 Edward E Pullée, *Leeds College of Art: Centenary Exhibition 1846-1946* (Leeds City Art Gallery, 1946)
29 *Yorkshire Evening Post* (25 July 1904)
30 Information from Bellis's daughter, Mrs Ruth Conder, a subsequent student at the Leeds School, and his colleague, David Barton, and *The Builder* (7 April and 7 July 1911)
31 Michael Parkin, *Percy Hague Jowett 1882-1955* (London: Michael Parkin Fine Art, 1974)
32 *Yorkshire Evening Post* (13 November 1905)
33 City of Leeds, 'Report of the Board of Education on the detailed inspection of the Leeds School of Art', *Education Committee Reports 1907-8 (Appendix A)*
34 City of Leeds Education Committee, *Art Exhibition no. 28: Notes and Suggestions for Teachers* (12 December 1908)
35 LI, *Official Handbook and Programme of Old English Autumn Fair: 7-10 October 1908*
36 Leeds School of Art, Department of Architecture, *Prospectus for the Session 1911-1912* (July 1911)
Derek Linstrum: *West Yorkshire Architects and Architecture* (London: Lund Humphries, 1978) p44
37 Sadler's time at Leeds and his artistic ideas and influence are fully described and discussed in:
Michael Sadler, *Michael Ernest Sadler (Sir Michael Sadler K.C.S.I.) 1861-1943: a memoir by his son* (London: Constable, 1949)
David Thistlewood, 'Expression and Design: the Leeds Arts Club debate on the Aesthetics of Modernism', in Hilary Diaper, (ed), *Michael Sadler* (Leeds: University Gallery, 1989) pp23-30
Michael Paraskos, 'Herbert Read in Leeds' in Benedict Read and David Thistlewood, (eds), *Herbert Read: a British Vision of World Art* (Leeds City Art Galleries, 1993) pp25-33
Steele, *op. cit.* note 26, pp177-95
38 Rutter's ideas, critical influence and impact on the Leeds art world are discussed in detail in: Frank Rutter, *Since I was Twenty-Five* (London: Constable, 1927) and Anna G Robins, *Modern Art in Britain 1910-1914* (London: Merrell Holberton with Barbican Art Gallery, 1997)
Thistlewood, *op. cit.* note 37
Steele, *op. cit.* note 26, pp177-95
39 Sadler, *op. cit.* note 37, pp265-7
40 Steele, *op. cit.* note 26, p.223
41 Tom Heron, *Paintings and Drawings by Bruce Turner* (Leeds: Leeds City Art Galleries, 1964)
42 John Roberts, (ed), *The Kramer Documents* (London: Valencia, 1983) pp17-19
Rachel Dickson, *William Roberts and Jacob Kramer: The Tortoise and the Hare* (London: Ben Uri Gallery, 2003)
Steele, *op. cit.* note 26, pp196-215
43 Sir Herbert Read in Millie Kramer (ed), *Jacob Kramer: a Memorial Volume* (Leeds: E J Arnold, 1969) p3, extracted from an address Read gave in Kramer's honour in 1960
44 Roberts, *op. cit.* note 42, p35
45 City of Leeds, *Education Committee Proceedings 1916-17* (7 December 1916)
46 City of Leeds, *Education Committee Proceedings 1918-19* and *1919-20*
47 Corinne Miller, 'The Leeds Table at the Royal College of Art', *Leeds Arts Calendar*, (1991) pp3-11
48 William Rothenstein, *A Plea for the Wider Use of Artists and Craftsmen*, (London: Constable, 1916) pp18-19
49 *Yorkshire Post* (20 May 1920)
Alexander Robertson, 'The Leeds Town Hall Decoration Scheme', *Leeds Arts Calendar*, (1974) pp16-22
Steele, *op. cit.* note 26, pp212-14
50 Roberts, *op. cit.* note 48, p80. Letter from Sadler (October 1921)
51 Eric Gill, *War Memorial* (Ditchling: St Domenic's Press, 1923)
Graham R Kent, 'Sadler, Gill and the Money Changers' in Diaper *op. cit.* note 37, pp34-8
52 *Yorkshire Post* (17 October 1923)
53 *Yorkshire Evening Post* (23 October 1922)
54 City of Leeds, *Education Committee Reports for 1921-2*, p20

Note on sources

The primary sources on the Leeds School of Art before 1920, which have been used by David Boswell, are as follows:
West Yorkshire Archive Service holds the records of the Leeds Mechanics Institute of Art, Science and Literature. For this study these comprise:
School of Art Sub-Committee *Minutes*
Leeds Institute *Annual Reports*
Leeds Institute *Calendars* (annual)
School of Art set of documents relating to the building and opening of the new School 1901-3
Several pamphlets relating to the history and activities of the School
Plans of the new School of Art submitted to the local authority

City of Leeds Central Library: Local and Family History holds copies of the City Council's published records and other relevant material as follows:
City of Leeds Education Committee *Reports* (annual) with separate appendices 1904-17
City of Leeds Education Committee *Proceedings* (annual) 1911-onwards
Newspaper Cutting Volumes (general and obituaries)
Several reports and exhibitions related to art education
Incomplete runs of Leeds Institute *Annual Reports* and *Calendars* from 1886-1902 and *Calendars* from 1899-1900 to 1905-6

Leeds Metropolitan University Archive although mainly relevant to the years after 1920, this includes:
Address by Ernest W Beckett MP at the opening of the new School of Art, 8 October 1903
Printed documents relating to the Leeds City Council takeover of the Institute's schools in 1906-7
Photographs (undated) of decorative metalwork made in the School's Design Department
A ceremonial trowel engraved LCC
Newspaper Cutting Volumes begun in 1922 for HH Holden

Leeds College of Art and Design Archive is mostly relevant to the years since 1993 but includes a few photographs of students and sets of plans of proposed and executed alterations to School building since the 1960s. Files on alumni are also in the course of creation.

Leeds City Art Gallery has its own artists' files and a large collection of artists' exhibition catalogues, in addition to the concise catalogues of their permanent collections, often published with the Henry Moore Centre for the Study of Sculpture.

Acknowledgements
I am grateful to the staff of these archives and libraries for their help, to Inés Plant for her research assistance, and to Ruth Conder, Michael Jackson, Derek Linstrum, Corinne Miller, Rachel Moss and Anne Levitt for specific information. Many more have helped with relevant parts of my earlier research and are thanked in: David M Boswell, *The Kitsons and the Arts* (University of York, unpublished DPhil. Thesis, 1995).

MATTHEW WITHEY, EVOLVING FORMS

1 John Hedgecoe and Henry Moore, *Henry Moore* (London: Thomas Nelson, 1968) p33
2 Leeds College of Art *Prospectus* (1923-4) p10
3 Roger Berthoud, *The Life of Henry Moore* (London and Boston: Faber & Faber, 1987) p57
4 Sally Festing, *Barbara Hepworth: a Life in Forms* (London: Penguin, 1995) p37
5 Hedgecoe and Moore, 1968, p33: 'For a whole year, I was Cotterill's only full-time student, and he looked after me like a child. He was always breathing down my neck, but, in a way, this was a help, because I got through the two-year course in one year. . . He did have part-time students, and evening classes, but I was his one real care.'
6 *Education* (24 October 1924)
7 The 16 July 1924 edition of the *Yorkshire Evening Post* reported on Moore's recent success in securing a travelling scholarship from the Royal College of Art
8 *Yorkshire Evening Post* (11 and 13 November 1924)

9 Jocelyn Horner first enrolled at Leeds School of Art in 1920, where she befriended Henry Moore. Her small collection of student works by Moore was bequeathed to Leeds City Art Gallery in 1973, together with a bust by Jacob Epstein, a sculptor Horner greatly admired. Another of Cotterill's students was Eric Rogers, who went on to the Royal College of Art in 1928, before establishing himself as an architectural sculptor in the Birmingham area, and a teacher at West Bromwich School of Art. In 1933, according to the *Yorkshire Evening News* (18 February 1933), he completed figures of *Architecture and Labour* for Wolverhampton's new technical college
10 *Yorkshire Evening News* (28 April 1927)
11 Leeds College of Art *Prospectus* (1927-8) p10
12 According to Susan James, the artists' daughter, Reginald Thomas Cotterill (1885-1966) stayed in York until his death. Ethel R Goldberg exhibited a sculpture called *Mourning Women* at the Society of Women Artists in London in 1929, but her artistic career thereafter seems to have been conducted on a part-time basis. Susan James emigrated to Canada in the 1956, taking with her whatever archive was left of her parents' careers, though David Manson, Ethel's cousin, does have a bust by Reginald and a small figure group by Ethel
13 *Yorkshire Evening Post* (1933)
14 John Rothenstein, *Yorkshire Evening Post* (21 September 1933)
15 This information comes from June Rey, the artist's widow
16 *Daily Telegraph* (16 January 1939)
17 *West London Press* (24 August 1962)
18 *Yorkshire Evening News* (4 November 1929)
19 *Yorkshire Post* (5 November 1929): 'Miss C Harrison shows two promising casts; a whimsical garden group of two little children timidly holding their first frog, and a more stately design of a bird-bath, set between two pillars and supported by lightly sleeping fauns. There is a strong, vigorous head of a lion, carved directly from stone, by Mr Maxwell Davidson, who also shows a carefully modelled and well-balanced nude study. One of the most striking exhibits of this section is a "memory composition" by a younger student, Mr T Allen, of a young shire colt. The artistic interpretation, the vigour and the essentially rhythmic movement are equally remarkable. The whole suggests the work of a student of no little talent.'
20 *Yorkshire Evening Post* (4 November 1929)
21 *Yorkshire Evening News* (19 November 1930), *Leeds Mercury* (15 July 1931) and *Yorkshire Evening Post* (21 July 1931)
22 *Leeds Mercury* (21 November 1931) and *Yorkshire Evening Post* (21 November 1931)
23 *Yorkshire Evening Post* (7 December 1932)
24 *Yorkshire Evening Post* (12 July 1932)
25 *Yorkshire Evening Post* (18 February 1932)
26 According to John Rothenstein, Sadler purchased Rey's *Mother and Child* (1931), a direct carving in Portland stone, after visiting the Yorkshire Artists' Exhibition in Leeds in 1932. He also owned bronze versions of Rey's heads of his wife and Jacob Kramer
27 Leeds College of Art *Prospectus* (1932-3) p10
28 *Yorkshire Evening Post* (29 November 1933). John Kavanagh (1903-1984), an Irishman from Cork, arrived in Leeds from the Royal College of Art, where he had been teaching. He studied for three years before that at the British School in Rome, having won the Prix de Rome for Sculpture in or around 1930. The *Yorkshire Weekly Post* (12 January 1924) described him as a former assistant to Charles Sargeant Jagger and a great admirer of Epstein. Coincidentally, according to the *Leeds Mercury* (16 November 1934), Percy Metcalfe – a former student of sculpture in Leeds – became Jagger's assistant soon after Kavanagh's recruitment
29 *Yorkshire Evening Post* (19 September 1936)
30 *Yorkshire Evening Post* (10 October 1935)
31 *Yorkshire Evening Post* (19 September 1936)
32 *Yorkshire Evening Post* (23 January 1939)
33 *Yorkshire Evening Post* (17 March 1939). Douglas Robertson Bissett (1908-fl1977) was born in Strichen, Aberdeenshire. He served his apprenticeship with an architectural sculptor in Glasgow, then enrolled in the city's art school. As well as a diploma, Bissett secured the Newbery Gold Medal and a John Keppie scholarship. He then served as an assistant teacher, before leaving Glasgow School of Art for a period of study in Germany in 1929. He went to Vienna in 1930, then to Copenhagen in 1933 where he studied under E Utzon Frank. Awarded a Rome sculpture scholarship in 1934, he spent a year in that city before moving on to the British School of Archaeology in Athens. At the time of his appointment to the sculpture department in Leeds, he was holding a similar post in Brighton.

INÉS PLANT, THE LEEDS EXPERIMENT

1 Edward E Pullée, Transcript of a telephone conversation, 27 June 1999 (Leeds College of Art and Design Archive) p1

2 Laurence Burt, Unpublished Memoirs, chapter 3, p28

3 *Leeds College of Art 1955*, (Bretton Hall Archive, HT/PL/41) p2

4 Harry Thubron, *Letter to Victor Pasmore*, 31 January 1980 (Bretton Hall Archive, HT/PL/18)

5 Chris Owen, *A Challenging Process; Forty Years of the Art and Design Foundation Course* (University of Huddersfield, 1999, unpublished MEd thesis) Appendix 1, p2

6 *Leeds College of Art 1955*, (Bretton Hall Archive, HT/PL/41) back of p2

7 *Leeds College of Art 1955*, (Bretton Hall Archive, HT/PL/41) p3

8 Eric Taylor, Harry Thubron, Norbert Lynton, *Basic Research*, (Leeds: Leeds College of Art, 1959) p8

9 Jon Thompson, 'Fond Memories of an Awkward Man', the Page Two article, *Art Monthly*, No. 90 (1985) p3

10 Mrs Elma Thubron: telephone conversation, 24 July 2000

11 *Leeds College of Art Thubron* (Bretton Hall Archive HT/PL/41) p1

12 Edward E Pullée, transcript of telephone conversation with Rebecca Lowe, 16 August 1999, p1

13 Taylor *et al, op. cit.* p3

14 Brian Godward, student and teacher Leeds College of Art, then at Leeds Polytechnic, interview, 23 July 2000

15 Leeds Education Committee *Minutes* (Leeds City Library Local Studies, ref. L352.23 L517)

16 John Jones, 'The New Spirit', *Gregory Fellowships in Painting and Sculpture* (Leeds: University of Leeds, 1986) p6

17 David Lewis (ed), *The Incomplete Circle: Eric Atkinson, Art and Education* (Aldershot: Scolar Press 2000) p69

18 Taylor *et al, op. cit.* p12

19 *Leeds College of Art 1955* (Bretton Hall Archive, HT/PL/41) p13

20 Lewis, *op. cit.,* note 17, p94

21 Lewis, *op. cit.,* note 17, p95

22 Robert Rowe, *Artefacts and Figures, The History of Leeds Art Galleries 1958-1983* (Brotherton Library, University of Leeds, Special Collections, unpublished manuscript, 96/004 part V)

23 Herbert Read,1893-1968, author, poet, art critic, lecturer, anarchist. Founder member ICA

24 Quoted in Herbert Read, *A Concise History of Modern Sculpture* (London: Thames and Hudson, 1979) cover

25 Jan Taylor, telephone conversation, 2 September 2000

26 Michael Pullée, telephone conversation, 1 August 2000

27 Herbert Read, *Education through Art*, (1943, 3rd ed. 1958), *Art and Industry* (1954)

28 Thompson, *op. cit.,* note 9 p2

29 Norbert Lynton, Letter, *New Statesman*, 2 March 1962

30 Harry Thubron, Letter to Victor Pasmore, 31 January 1980 (Bretton Hall Archive, HT/PL/18)

31 Maurice de Sausmarez, *Basic Design: the dynamics of visual form* (London: Studio Vista, Van Nostrand, 1964) p5

32 de Sausmarez, *op. cit.* p7

33 Anton Ehrenzweig, *The Hidden Order of Art: A Study in the Psychology of Artistic Imagination*, (London: Weidenfeld and Nicolson, 1967) p148

34 David Thistlewood, *A Continuing Process: The New Creativity in British Art Education, 1955-1965* (London: Institute of Contemporary Arts, 1981)

35 Lewis, *op. cit.,* note 17

36 *Yorkshire Evening Post*, 13 July 1968

37 Jan Taylor, *Art and Life, Eric Taylor, 1909-1999* (Huddersfield: New Light Gallery, 2000) p6

CHRIS OWEN, FIRM FOUNDATIONS

1 The term 'Basic Design Movement' is used throughout this article to identify the work of the group of art education reformers who worked together intermittently in the mid-1950s, and included Harry Thubron and Tom Hudson in Leeds and Victor Pasmore and Richard Hamilton in Newcastle. The term was never accepted by Thubron, who preferred 'Basic Research' to 'Basic Design'. The term is used here for convenience, and is not intended to contradict research which has identified clear differences of emphasis in the pedagogy of these individual pioneers – see, for example, RR Yeomans, *The Foundation Course of Victor Pasmore and Richard Hamilton* (PhD Thesis, London Institute of Education, 1987); E Forrest, 'Harry Thubron at Leeds, and Views on the Value of his Ideas for Education Today', *Journal of Art and Design Education*, volume 4, no. 2 (1985), pp147-167

2 NACAE, *First Report of the National Advisory Council on Art Education,* (The First Coldstream Report), (London: DES, 1960) p1

3 NACAE *op. cit.*

4 Leeds College of Art, *Student Prospectus* (1958)

5 LCAD *op. cit.*

6 NACAE, *First Report of the National Advisory Council on Art Education*, Addendum (London: DES, 1965) p2

7 Derek Carruthers, *Synopsis of Foundation Phase and Materials and Processes Courses*, (Leicester College of Art and Design, 1966). Typescript in NAEA, Bretton Hall; RCA, *Aims of a Foundation Year Course* (London: Royal College of Art, undated). Typescript in NAEA, Bretton Hall

8 Tom Hudson, *Foundation Studies* (Leicester College of Art and Design? undated). Typescript in NAEA, Bretton Hall

9 Yeomans, *op. cit.* pp176-7

10 L Jobey, 'The Man Who Took Art Back to Basics' (*Sunday Times*, January 1985)

11 Chris Owen, *A Challenging Process; Forty Years of the Art and Design Foundation Course* (University of Huddersfield, 1999, unpublished MEd thesis) Appendix 1

12 NACAE *op. cit.* p2

13 NACAE *op. cit.* p2

14 NACAE/NCDAD, *The Structure of Art Education* (The Second Coldstream Report) Joint Report (London: DES 1970) p15

15 Eric Taylor, Statement to Teaching Staff, Announcing his Resignation (Leeds College of Art and Design, 1971) Typescript

16 NCDAD Memorandum: *DipAD courses; the Future Preparation and Entry of Students* (London: DES, 1973) paragraph 4

17 NCDAD *op. cit.* paragraph 9

18 Edexcel/NBFSAD *Foundation Art and Design Regional Forums* (London, June 1999) Conference Papers p14

19 Edexcel *BTEC Diploma in Foundation Studies (Art and Design)* (London: Edexcel, 2000) p6

20 Edexcel, *op. cit.* p33

21 Yeomans, *op. cit.* p192

22 David Thistlewood, *A Continuing Process: The New Creativity in British Art Education 1955-65* (London: Institute of Contemporary Arts, 1981) p4